Learn to Read Biblical Hebrew

Jeff A. Benner.

d Biblical Hebrew," by Jeff A. Benner.
584-0.

by Virtualbookworm.com Publishing Inc.,
, College Station, TX 77845, US. ©2003,
All rights reserved. Any part of this book
l for educational purposes only, without
n.

n the United States of America.

Learn t

A gui
alphab
struc

~~~~~~~

Cover design by

"Learn to Re
ISBN 1-58939

Published 200
P.O. Box 994
Jeff A. Benne
may be copie
prior permissi

Manufactured

Table of Contents

To my Father who set me on the
path of Biblical studies

Introduction

Why Learn Hebrew?

A translation of the Biblical text is a translator's "interpretation" of the text. The translator's beliefs will often influence how the text will be translated and anyone using his translation is seeing it through his eyes rather than the original authors. Only by studying the original language of the Bible can one see the text in its original state.

Learning the Hebrew language can be both fun and exciting. By simply studying the pages that follow, for just a few minutes a day, you will soon be reading Hebrew, build a Hebrew vocabulary and even begin translating Biblical passages for your self.

About Hebrew

The English word "alphabet" is derived from the first two letters of the Greek Alphabet--Alpha and Beta. Hebrew on the other hand, uses the word "alephbet," the first two letters of the Hebrew alephbet--aleph and bet. The Hebrew alephbet consists of 22 consonants. The vowels (called nikkudot, nikkud in the singular) are dots and dashes added above and below the consonants. One advantage to Hebrew is that the sound for each letter remains consistent, unlike English where one has to memorize many variations. For instance, the word circus contains the letter "c" twice, the first time it is pronounced like an "S" while the second time it is pronounced like a "K." In Hebrew, the letter כ is always pronounced as a "K."

Unlike English, which is read from left to right, Hebrew is read from right to left just as many other Semitic languages do including Aramaic and Arabic. This may sound difficult at first but in a very short time you will get used to it.

When sounding out a word, it will be easier if you remember the Consonant (C) and Vowel (V) patterns of Hebrew words. In English, the consonants and vowels may be arranged in any order, such as in the word "circle" which has a C+V+C+C+C+V pattern. Hebrew on the other hand, is very consistent, and each word will usually follows a C+V+C+V+C... pattern. The Hebrew word מֶלֶךְ (melek - king) contains the pattern C+V+C+V+C, מֶלְכוֹ (meleko – his king) is C+V+C+V+C+V and הַמֶּלֶךְ (hamelek – the king) is C+V+C+V+C+V+C.

The pronunciations of some of the consonants and vowels have changed over the centuries but this does not affect the meaning of words as the letters of the words define it, and not the sounds. We will learn to pronounce them according to the Modern Hebrew pronunciation. Modern Hebrew pronunciation is also divided into two parts, Ashkenazi and Sephardic. Since Sephardic is the pronunciation adopted by the Modern State of Israel, we will use this pronunciation.

About this Book

When I began to study the Hebrew language I used several different resources but found that they were not compiled in a format for beginning Hebrew students. I began to arrange charts and lists with the necessary information as a ready resource for learning and reading the Hebrew Bible.

This book is the result. Included in this book are lessons for learning the alephbet, verbs, nouns, adjectives and sentence structure.

If at any time you have questions about the Ancient Hebrew Research Center, this book, its content or the lessons, please feel free to E-mail your questions or comments to us through our web site;

http://www.ancient-hebrew.org

Additional Resources

It should be kept in mind that this book is not meant to be used for in-depth Biblical study, but as a reference guide for Biblical reading practice, vocabulary building and sentence comprehension. More specific dictionaries and lexicons will be necessary for more in-depth study.

Through the process of Hebraic studies, you will want to dig deeper into the meaning of specific words and phrases. At this point the purchase of a Hebrew Bible and a Hebrew Lexicon will be helpful. There are several different kinds of Hebrew Bibles. The standard Hebrew Bible will be a Bible written only in Hebrew. The Interlinear Bible will have the Hebrew on one line and the English translation for each word under each Hebrew word. A Parallel Bible will have the Hebrew text on one page and the English translation on the other

There are several different Lexicons but be sure that the one you purchase includes all the words of the Bible with the prefixes and suffixes attached. This will allow you to look up a word even if you do not know the root. I recommend Benjamin Davidson's *Hebrew and Chaldee Lexicon of the Bible*.

Part 1
The Alephbet

Each of following eleven lessons introduces two new consonants and may or many not introduce new vowels. Each lesson will also include a practice section, new vocabulary words and sentences. The practice session will allow you to practice the new letters and vowels and refresh yourself on old ones. The vocabulary section will consist of a few words using the new letters and vowels to begin building your Hebrew vocabulary. The Sentences will allow you to begin using your new words in sentences.

To assist you in learning the letters and words, I recommend that you put the letters and words you are learning on flashcards so that you can study them at any time.

Transliterations of each of the lessons are provided at the end of the lessons to assist with pronunciation. When reading these transliterations, remember to use the correct Hebrew sound for each vowel. For example the transliterated Hebrew vowel sound "o" is the long "o" sound as in the English word "rope."

Alephbet and Vowels

The following is a chart of all the consonants in the
Hebrew Alephbet. This chart includes all the variations
for each letter. For example the letter beyt can be written
as בּ or ב. Several of the letters have a final form as well
and are also included (such as מ and ם).

Lamed	ל	Aleph	א
Mem	מ ם	Beyt	בּ ב
Nun	נ ן	Gimel	ג
Samech	ס	Dalet	ד
Ayin	ע	Hey	ה
Pey	פ פּ ף	Vav	ו
Tsade	צ ץ	Zayin	ז
Quph	ק	Chet	ח
Resh	ר	Tet	ט
Shin	שׁ שׂ	Yud	י
Tav	ת	Kaph	כ כּ ך ךּ

The Vowels

Below are the names for each of the Hebrew vowels. The letter aleph is used below to show the placement of each vowel and is not part of the vowel.

Cholam maley	וֹ	Qamats	אָ
Qubbuts	אֻ	Patach	אַ
Shuruq	וּ	Segol	אֶ
Chataph qamats	אֳ	Tsere	אֵ
Chataph patach	אֲ	Sh'va	אְ
Chataph segol	אֱ	Chireq	אִ
		Cholam	אֹ

Letter Comparisons

Several of the Hebrew letters are very similar and at the beginning they are easily confused with other letters that look alike. Below is a chart showing letters of similarity in order to make the reader familiar with the slight differences.

Beyt	ב	Dalet	ד	Kaph	כ
Kaph	כ	Resh	ר	Pey	פ
Beyt	ב	Vav	ו	Mem	מ
Pey	פ	Zayin	ז	Tet	ט
Gimel	ג	Vav	ו	F. Mem	ם
Nun	נ	F. Nun	ן	Samech	ס
Hey	ה	Zayin	ז	Samech	ס
Chet	ח	F. Nun	ן	Tet	ט
Hey	ה	Chet	ח	Ayin	ע
Tav	ת	Tav	ת	Tsade	צ

Lesson 1 – aleph, beyt

Consonants

א   The "Aleph" is the first letter of the Hebrew alephbet. This consonant is silent.

ב   The "Beyt" is pronounced two ways, a "b" as in "ball," and as "v" as in "visit." When a dagesh (a dot in the middle of the letter) appears in the middle of the letter (בּ) it will have the "b" sound. When the letter appears without the dagesh (ב) the letter is pronounced "v."

Vowels

אָ   This vowel, "qamats," (the little "T" shaped mark under the aleph) is pronounced "ah" as in "father."

אַ   This vowel, "patach," is also pronounced "ah" as in "father."

Practice

בָ אַ אָ בָ אַ אָ בַ בָ אַ בַ :1

אָבָ בַ אָבָ אַ בַּ אָ בָ :2

15

Vocabulary

2: בָּא - Came   1: אָב - Father

Sentences

1:   אָב בָּא - Father came.

Lesson 2 – Mem, Yud

Consonants

מ   The "Mem" is pronounced "m" as in "mother."

ם   The "final Mem" is used only when it appears at the end of a word. The pronunciation does not change.

י   The "Yud" is pronounced "y" as in "yes." (When the "yud" is suffixed to a word it means "of me" or "my." Sentence #2 includes the word אָב - father, with the suffix י forming the word אָבִי - my father.)

Vowels

אִ   The "chireq" is pronounced "ee" as in "bee."

אֵ   The "tsere" is pronounced "ey" as in "grey."

Practice

1: בְ בֶ בֵ בַ אֵ אֶ מַ מֶ מָ סָ מַ

2: אֵ אֵ בִי בִ בִי מִי אֵם אִם

Vocabulary

2: מִי - Who   1: אֵם - Mother

Sentences

1: מִי בָא - Who came?

2: אָבִי בָא - My father came.

Lesson 3 – Nun, Hey

Consonants

נ
The "Nun" is pronounced "n" as in "no."

ן
The "final Nun" is only used when it appears at the end of a word. The pronunciation does not change.

ה
The "Hey" is pronounced "h" as in "hello." (When the letter ה is prefixed to a word it means "the" such as in sentence #6 where the letter ה is prefixed to the word נָבִיא - prophet, forming הַנָבִיא - the prophet.)

Practice

‎1: הָ הַ הִ הֵ הַ נַ נִ נֵ בֶּן בָּה הַב

‎2: הַן הֵן נָה נִה נֵה נָב מָה מִן נָא

‎3: הִי הִיא נִי נִיא נֵי הֵי הֵן ¹נָבָה בָּנָה

---

¹ Hebrew words with more than one syllable usually accent the final syllables pronouncing the final Consonant-Vowel-Consonant as one syllable. For instance, the word אֲנִי, in the vocabulary list, is pronounced "a-niy" rather than "an-iy."

Vocabulary

2: אֲנִי - I		1: אֵי – Where
4: בֵּן - Son		3: הִיא – She
6: נָבִיא - Prophet		5: בָּאָה - came (f.)
		7: מָה or מֶה - What

Sentences

1: מִי הִיא - Who [is][2] she?
2: בְּנִי בָּא - My son came.
3: אֲנִי אָב - I [am a][3] father.
4: אֵי אָבִי - Where [is] my father?
5: מָה נָבִיא - What [is a] prophet?
6: הַנָּבִיא בָּא - The[4] prophet came.

---

[2] The English verb "to be" and its various tenses (am, is, are, etc.) do not exist in Hebrew and need to be added in the translation.

[3] English has two indefinite articles, "a" and "an" which also do not exist in Hebrew and must be added in the translation.

[4] When the letter ה is prefixed to a word it means "the" such as in sentence #6 where the letter ה is prefixed to the word נָבִיא (prophet) forming הַנָּבִיא, meaning "the prophet."

Lesson 4 – Lamed, Vav

Consonants

ל   The "Lamed" is pronounced "l" as in "<u>l</u>ong."

ו   The "Vav" is pronounced "v" as in "<u>v</u>isit."

Vowels

אְ   The "sh'va" is pronounced "eh" as in "h<u>e</u>lp" when it is placed under the first letter of the word. When this vowel appears anywhere else in the word, it is usually a "syllable break" and not pronounced.

אֶ   The "segol" is pronounced "eh" as in "h<u>e</u>lp."

Practice

1: לְ לַ לֶ לְ לְ לֶ וּ וְ וִ וִ לִ לֵ לִ לֵ⁵ וֵ וִ

2: וִ וָ לְל וְל וֶל וַל לֶה הֶל לֶה לָה הֶל

3: וַיִם לָבָה לַיְל לְבָמָה מְלֹא

---

⁵ When one of the "a" vowels (qamats or patach) is followed by the consonant "yud" in the same syllable, the pronunciation is a long "i" as in "lie" and NOT "ay" as in "lay."

Learn to Read Biblical Hebrew

Vocabulary

God - אֵל‎ :2	Night - לַיְלָה‎ :1
Believe - אָמֵן‎ :4	Water - מַיִם‎ :3
Sea - יָם‎ :6	Here - הִנֵּה‎[6] :5

Sentences

:1 לַיְלָה בָּא‎ - Night came.

:2 מַיִם בַּיָּם‎[7] - Water [is] in the sea.

:3 בְּנִי בָּא לִי‎[8] - My son came to me.

:4 בָּאָה‎[9] בַּלַּיְלָה‎ - Mother came in the night. אֵם

:5 אָבִי וְאִמִּי‎[10] הִנֵּה

---

[6] When the dagesh (the dot in the middle of a letter) is placed within some letters, such as in the nun in the word הִנֵּה, it doubles the letter. Therefore, this word is pronounced "hin-ney" rather than "hi-ney."

[7] When the letter "beyt" is prefixed to a word it means "in" as in sentence #4 - בַּלַּיְלָה - in the night.)

[8] When the letter "lamed" is used as a prefix it means "to" or "for."

[9] The vocabulary word בָּאָה (she came) is the feminine form of the masculine verb בָּא (he came) which was given in lesson one.

[10] When the letter "vav" is prefixed to a word it means "and."

22

My father and my mother [are] here. -

Lesson 5 – Resh, Shin

Consonants

ר   The "Resh" is pronounced "r" as in "rain."

שׁ   The "Shin" is pronounced two ways, "sh" as in "sharp," and "s" as in "sign." When a dot is placed on the top right corner of the letter (שׁ) it takes the "sh" sound and when the dot is placed on the top left corner of the letter (שׂ) it takes the "s" sound.

Vowels

וֹ   This consonant (vav) / vowel (cholam) combination is called a "cholam maley" and is pronounced "ow" as in "open."

Practice

1: שׁוֹ שׂוֹ רוֹ שִׂי שִׁי רִי רֶ שֶׂ שַׂ שֶׁ

2: רוֹשׁ רֶשׁ שָׂר שׂוֹר שִׁיר שַׂר שֵׁשׁ

3: שֶׁל הֵשׁ שִׂים שָׁב מְשׁ רַב יַר נֵר בָּר

Vocabulary

2: שָׁמַיִם - Heaven   1: שָׁלוֹם - Peace

4: בָּרָא - Created (m)   3: אָמַר - Said (m)

6: אָמְרָה - Said (f)   5: שֵׁם - Name

8: יוֹם - Day   7: שַׂר - Ruler

10: רַבִּי - Rabbi   9: אוֹר - Light

Sentences

1: שַׂר שָׁלוֹם - Ruler of Peace.

2: יוֹם וְלַיְלָה - Day and night.

3: שְׁמִי לֵוִי - My name [is] Levi.

4: מַה שְׁמוֹ[11] - What [is] his name?

5: שְׁמוֹ אַבְרָהָם - His name [is] Abraham.

6: בָּרָא אֵל[12] שָׁמַיִם - God created heaven.

7: אָמַר רַבִּי לִי שָׁלוֹם

Rabbi said to me Shalom. -

___

[11] When the consonant/vowel combination "cholam maley" is suffixed to a word it means "of him" or "his."

[12] In Hebrew, the verb usually appears before the object of the verb.

Lesson 6 – Ayin, Tet

Consonants

עַ   The "Ayin" is also a silent (the same as the aleph).

ט   The "Tet" is pronounced "t" as in "tune."

Vowels

וְ   This consonant (vav) / vowel combination is called a "shuruq" and is pronounced "uw" as in "tune."

Practice

1: עָ טֶ עֲ טִ עַ טָ עֵ אָט טוּ טֵ אָ טֵא עֵא עֶט טֵע

2: הוּ הוּ אוֹ אוּ בוֹ בוּ לוֹ לוּ רוּ רוּ וֹן וּן

3: רֵט שֵׁט בֵּע בֵּט שׁוּל טוֹב טוּב טוּע עוּט

Vocabulary

Evening – עֶרֶב :2	Good - טוֹב :1
Israel - יִשְׂרָאֵל :4	Over, on - עַל :3
She - הִיא :6	He - הוּא :5
	Keep (m) - שׁוֹמֵר :7

Sentences

1: עֶרֶב טוֹב[13] - Good evening.

2: מַה שְׁמָם[14] - What is their name?

3: שְׁמוּ יִשְׂרָאֵל - Their name is Israel.

4: שָׁלוֹם עַל יִשְׂרָאֵל - Peace over Israel.

5: מִי בָּא עֶרֶב - Who came in the evening?

6: הוּא בָּא בָּעֶרֶב - He came in the evening.

7: הִיא בָּאָה בָּעֶרֶב - She came in the evening.

---

[13] In Hebrew, the adjective proceeds the noun, such as word טוֹב (good) which comes after עֶרֶב (evening).

[14] When the letter "Mem" is suffixed to a noun it means "of them" or "their."

Lesson 7 – Tav, Dalet

Consonants

תּ   The "Tav" is pronounced "t" as in "tune."

ד   The "Dalet" is pronounced "d" as in "dig."

Vowels

אֶ   This vowel combination (sh'va and segol) is called a "chataph segol" and is pronounced "eh" as in "help."

אֹ   The "cholam" is pronounced "o" as in "open."

Practice

1: דַּ תִ תֶ תֶ דוֹ ד דַ דָ דֶ דֶ דֶ

2: דַּד דֶת דָת תֶּד תֵּד תֹד דוֹת דֹת דֶת דָת

3: מִיד תַּן מֹת אֶל דָב בַּת בֵּית תּוֹד

Vocabulary

2: מֹשֶׁה[15] - Moses
4: אֶת[16] - (With)
6: שַׁבָּת - Sabbath

1: אֱלֹהִים - God
3: נָתַן - Gave (m)
5: תּוֹרָה[17] - Teaching

8: תַּלְמִידָה
Student (f) -

7: תַּלְמִיד - Student (m)

10: לוֹמֶדֶת
Studies (f) -

9: לוֹמֵד - Studies (m)

11: רֵאשִׁית[18]

---

[15] Remembering the C+V+C+V rule, the Hebrew word for Moses, מֹשֶׁה, appears to be missing a vowel after the "mem." Since Hebrew requires a vowel after each consonant, the vowel is the "cholam" and is placed above the letter "shin" in the same place as the dot above the right leg of the shin. The dot in this case serves two purposes.

[16] The Hebrew word אֶת is occasionally used in the text to mean "with" but is more frequently used (about 7,000 times) as a marker for the direct object of the verb and is untranslatable into English. For example, in the sentence; "I made the dinner"; the phrase "the dinner" is the direct object and would be preceded by the word אֶת. If the sentence were; "I made a dinner," אֶת would not precede it since "dinner" in this sentence is not a direct object.

[17] The word תּוֹרָה, while often translated as "law," actually means "teaching" and is also the Hebrew name for the first five books of the Bible as they contain the "teachings" of God.

[18] An exception to the rule requiring the C+V+C+V pattern is the word רֵאשִׁית. The aleph does not always require a vowel after it.

Sentences

1: שַׁבָּת שָׁלוֹם - Peaceful Sabbath.

2: וְשָׁמְרוּ אֶת הַשַּׁבָּת

And they will keep the Sabbath. -

3: בְּרֵאשִׁית בָּרָא אֱלֹהִים

In the beginning God created. -

4: תַּלְמִידָה לוֹמֶדֶת תּוֹרה

A student studies Torah. -

5: נָתַן מֹשֶׁה ¹⁹לָנוּ אֶת הַתּוֹרָה

Moses gave to us the Torah. -

6: תַּלְמִיד לוֹמֵד אֶת הַתּוֹרָה

A student studies the Torah. -

---

[19] When the letter "lamed" is used as a prefix it means "to" or "for." The suffix נוּ means "us." combined, this prefix and suffix mean "to us."

Learn to Read Biblical Hebrew

Lesson 8 – Tsade, Quph

Consonants

צ   The "Tsade" is pronounced "ts" as in "po<u>ts</u>."

ץ   The "final Tsade" is used when this letter appears at the end of a word. The pronunciation does not change.

ק   The "Quph" is pronounced "q" as in "<u>q</u>uiet."

Vowels

אֲ   This vowel combination (sh'va and patach) is called a "chataph patach" and is pronounced "ah" as in "f<u>a</u>ther."

31

Learn to Read Biblical Hebrew

Practice

1: צֶ צֵ צֶ צָ צֵ צָ קֵ קֵ קָ קַ קֵ קֵ

2: אֵץ אֵץ קֵץ צֵץ צֶק צֵק קֵץ קֵץ רַק רֵץ

3: צִי קִי צֵא צֶא צֹה קַא קֹה קֶא קֹה הַץ

Vocabulary

2: אֶרֶץ - Land   1: הָיָה - existed (m)

Sentences - Genesis 1:14[20]

וַיֹּאמֶר אֱלֹהִים יְהִי מְאֹרֹת בִּרְקִיעַ
הַשָּׁמַיִם בֵּין הַיּוֹם וּבֵין הַלַּיְלָה וְהָיוּ
לְהַבְדִּיל לְאֹתֹת וּלְמוֹעֲדִים וּלְיָמִים
וְשָׁנִים

---

[20] From this point on the alephbet lessons will include Biblical passages. While most of the words will not be recognizable at this time, remember that our objective is to "read" the text, not necessarily understand it.

Lesson 9 – Chet, Kaph

Consonants

ח The "Chet" is pronounced "ch" as in the German word "i<u>ch</u>" or the name "Ba<u>ch</u>."

כ The "Kaph" is pronounced two ways, "k" as in kick, and "kh" as in the German word "i<u>ch</u>" or the name "Ba<u>ch</u>." If the dagesh appears in the middle of the letter (כּ) it is pronounced "k." When the dagesh does not appear in the letter (כ) it is pronounced "kh."

ך The "final kaph" may also appear with the dagesh (ךּ) or without the dagesh (ך) with the pronunciations being the same as the "kaph." All words will end with a consonant, the only exception to this is the "final kaph" which will usually be followed by a vowel.

Vowels

 The "qubbuts" is pronounced "u" as in "t<u>u</u>ne."

Practice

1: כַּ כָ כֹ כֶּ כֵ כֶ חֶ חֵ חָ ח

2: חַךּ כֹח כָח חֵךּ חֵךּ כֹח

3: רֹח רֶח רֹךּ אַךּ חַךּ אָח

Vocabulary

2: עֵשֶׂב - Grass, herb   1: כֵּן - Yes, so

4: נֹחַ[21] – Noah   3: עֵץ - Tree

Sentences - Genesis 1:5

וַיִּקְרָא אֱלֹהִים לָאוֹר יוֹם וְלַחֹשֶׁךְ קָרָא
לָיְלָה וַיְהִי־עֶרֶב וַיְהִי־בֹקֶר יוֹם אֶחָד

---

[21] According to the standard form of Hebrew pronunciation the name

נֹחַ should be pronounced "nocha" but, when the patach vowel appears below the letter "chet" at the end of a word, the two sounds trade places and is in fact pronounced "no'ach." This is unique only to this letter and vowel combination.

Lesson 10 – Zayin, Pey

Consonants

ז   The "Zayin" is pronounced "z" as in "zebra."

פ   The "Pey" is pronounced two ways, "p" as in "pad," and "ph" as "phone." If the dagesh appears in the middle of the letter (פ) it is pronounced "p." When the dagesh does not appear in the letter (פ) it is pronounced "ph."

ף   The "final Pey" is only used when this letter appears at the end of a word. The "final pey" will never appear with the dagesh and will therefore be pronounced "ph."

Vowels

אָ   This vowel combination (sh'va and qamats) is called a "chataph qamats" and is pronounced "ah" as in "father."

Practice

1: זוֹ זִ זָ זֶ פֹ פֶ פֵ פֶ פָ פֶ

2: זֵף פֵז זָא הַז אֹז אַף זָא זֶה

3: קֵף זֵף כַף שֵׁז שָׁו פֹם פֵח

Vocabulary

1: אֲשֶׁר - Which, who   2: עָשָׂה - To do, make

3: פָּנִים - Face

Sentences - Genesis 1:11

וַיֹּאמֶר אֱלֹהִים תַּדְשֵׁא הָאָרֶץ דֶּשֶׁא עֵשֶׂב
מַזְרִיעַ זֶרַע עֵץ פְּרִי עֹשֶׂה פְּרִי לְמִינוֹ
אֲשֶׁר זַרְעוֹ־בוֹ עַל־הָאָרֶץ וַיְהִי־כֵן

36

Lesson 11 – Gimel, Samech

Consonants

גּ   The "Gimel" is pronounced "g" as in "game."

ס   The "Samech" is pronounced "s" as in "sand."

Practice

1:    סַ סֶ סֵ סִ סָ סְ גֶ גֵ גִ גָ גַ גְ

2:    הֶס אָס סֵה גֹוא אַג גָא גֹה גֵה

3:    סֹח מַס סֵם סֶף סַג נַס סֵר סֹד

Vocabulary

1: כָּל²² - All   2: אָדָם - Man

3: עוֹף - Bird   4: דָּגָה - Fish

---

²² This word appears to be pronounced "kal" but, is actually pronounced "kol." In this one instance the qamats vowel represents a rare vowel pronounced "o."

Sentences - Genesis 1:26

וַיֹּאמֶר אֱלֹהִים נַעֲשֶׂה אָדָם בְּצַלְמֵנוּ
כִּדְמוּתֵנוּ וְיִרְדּוּ בִדְגַת הַיָּם וּבְעוֹף
הַשָּׁמַיִם וּבַבְּהֵמָה וּבְכָל־הָאָרֶץ וּבְכָל־
הָרֶמֶשׂ הָרֹמֵשׂ עַל־הָאָרֶץ

Lesson Transliterations

Lesson 1
P1: bah ah vah bah ah ah bah ah ah vah
P2: vah bah ahv bah ahv bah
V1: ahv
V2: bah
S1: ahv bah

Lesson 2
P1: vee bey vey bee ey ee mee mey mah mah
P2: ey ee vee bee mee eym eem
V1: eym
V2: mee
S1: mee bah
S2: ah-vee bah

Lesson 3
P1: hah hah hee hey nah nee ney ney beyn bah hahv
P2: hahn heyn nah nee ney nahv mah meen nah
P3: hee hee nee nee ney hey heen nah-vah bah-nah
V1: ey
V2: ah-nee
V3: hee
V4: beyn
V5: bah-ah
V6: nah-vee
V7: mah
S1: mee hee
S2: bey-nee bah
S3: ah-nee ahv
S4: ey ah-vee
S5: mah nah-vee

S6:   hah-nah-vee bah

Lesson 4
P1:   ley lah leh lee lah veh vah vee lie lee lie vie vey
P2:   vehv vahv leyl vehl veyl vahl ley heyl lah hahl
P3:   vah-veem lee-bah lah-yeel leyv-mah mah-ley
V1:   lie-lah
V2:   eyl
V3:   mah-yeem
V4:   ah-meyn
V5:   hee-ney
V6:   yahm
S1:   lie-lah bah
S2:   mah-yeem bah-yahm
S3:   bey-nee bah lee
S4:   eym bah-ah bah-lie-lah
S5:   ah-vee veh-ey-mee hee-ney

Lesson 5
P1:   sheh shah sey rey ree rie shey sehy row show sow
P2:   sheysh sahr sheer showr seer rahsh rowsh
P3:   bahr neyr yahr rahv meesh sahv seem heysh shehl
V1:   shah-lowm
V2:   shah-mah-yeem
V3:   ah-mahr
V4:   bah-rah
V5:   sheym
V6:   ahm-rah
V7:   sahr
V8:   yowm
V9:   owr
V10: rah-bee
S1:   sahr shah-lowm
S2:   yowm veh-lie-lah
S3:   sh'mee ley-vee

S4:   mah sh'mow
S5:   sh'mow ahv-rah-hahm
S6:   bah-rah eyl shah-mah-yeem
S7:   ah-mahr rah-bee lee shah-lowm

Lesson 6

P1:   eh teh ey tee ee eht tuw teh eh eht teh
P2:   how huw ow uw bow buw low luw ruw own uwn
P3:   reht seht beh veht shuwl tuwv tuw uwt
V1:   towv
V2:   eh-rehv
V3:   ahl
V4:   yees-rah-eyl
V5:   huw
V6:   hee
V7:   show-meyr
S1:   eh-rehv towv
S2:   mah sh'muw
S3:   sh'muw yees-rah-eyl
S4:   shah-lowm ahl yees-rah-eyl
S5:   mee bah eh-rehv
S6:   huw bah bah-eh-rehv
S7:   hee bah-ah bah-eh-rehv

Lesson 7

P1:   deh dah deh dey dee dah dow dow teh teh tey tee tah
P2:   daht deht dowt dowt towd tehd deht deyt dahd
P3:   towd veyt vaht dahv ehl mowt tahn meed
V1:   eh-low-heem
V2:   mow-sheh
V3:   rey-sheet
V4:   eht
V5:   tahl-meed
V6:   tahl-mee-dah
V7:   low-meyd

V8:   low-meh-deht
V9:   tow-rah
V10: shah-baht
V11: nah-tahn
S1:   shah-baht shah-lowm
S2:   veh-shahm-ruw eht hah-shah-baht
S3:   beh-rey-sheet bah-rah eh-low-heem
S4:   tahl-mee-dah low-meh-deht tow-rah
S5:   nah-tahn mow-sheh lah-nuw eht hah-tow-rah
S6:   tahl-meed low-meyd eht hah-tow-rah

Lesson 8

P1:   tsey tsah tsah tsow tsah tseh qee qow qah qah qeh qah
P2:   ehts owts qeyts tsahq tseeq qeets qowts rahq rehts
P3:   tsey qee tsey tseh tsow qah qah qow howts
V1:   hah-yah
V2:   eh-rehts
S1:   vie-yow-mehr eh-low-heem yeh-hee meh-ow-rowt beer-qee-ah hah-shah-mah-yeem beyn hah-yowm uw-veyn hah-lie-lah veh-hie-uw leh-hahv-deel leh-owt-owt uwl-mow-ah-deem uwl-yah-meem veh-shah-neem

Lesson 9

P1:   kah khah kee kheh key khuw cheh chey chee chow
P2:   chahkh kow-ahch khahch chey-khah cheykh keech
P3:   row-ahch ruw-ahch rahk ahkh chah-khah ahch
V1:   keyn
V2:   eh-sehv
V3:   eyts
V4:   now-ahch
S1:   vie-yeeq-rah eh-low-heem lah-owr yowm veh-lah-chow-shehkh qah-rah lie-lah vie-hee eh-rehv vie-hee vow-qehr yowm eh-chahd

Lesson 10

P1: pheh pah peh phey pah pow zuw zey zah zee zow

P2: zeh zey ahph eyz hehz zeh phahz zehph

P3: pow-ahch pahm sahz shahz kahph zeykh quwph

V1: ah-shehr

V2: ah-sah

V3: pah-neem

S1: vie-yow-mehr eh-low-heem tahd-shey hah-ah-rehts deh-sheh ey-sehv mahz-ree-ah zeh-rah eyts peh-ree ow-seh peh-ree leh-mee-now ah-shehr zahr-ow vow ahl hah-ah-rehts vie-hee kheyn

Lesson 11

P1: sow suw sah sey see geh gah geh gow gee gah gah

P2: hehs ahs sey gow ahg geh gow gah

P3: sow-ahch mahs seym seyph seyg gahs suwr sowd

V1: kowl

V2: ah-dahm

V3: owph

V4: dah-gah

S1: vie-yow-mehr eh-low-heem nah-ah-seh ah-dahm beh-tsahl-mey-nuw hah-reh-mehs veh-yeer-duw veed-gaht hah-yowm uwv-owph hah-shah-mah-yeem keed-muw-tey-nuw uwv-khowl hah-ah-rehts uwv-khowl uw-vah-beh-hey-mah hah-row-meys ahl hah-ah-rehts

Part 2
Reading Practice

Below is the first chapter of the book of Genesis in Hebrew. The name "Genesis" comes from the Greek name for this book and means "origins." The Hebrew name for this book is "Bereshiyt." The Hebrew names for the first five books of the Bible is derived from the first word (or first principle word) of the book. In this case, the first word in the book is "bereshiyt" and means "in the beginning."

The purpose of this section is to allow you to practice reading. Also included is a transliteration of the chapter for pronunciation help. Again, remember to use the correct Hebrew pronunciation for each vowel.

The Hebrew

1 בְּרֵאשִׁית בָּרָא אֱלֹהִים אֵת הַשָּׁמַיִם וְאֵת הָאָרֶץ

2 וְהָאָרֶץ הָיְתָה תֹהוּ וָבֹהוּ וְחֹשֶׁךְ עַל־פְּנֵי תְהוֹם
וְרוּחַ אֱלֹהִים מְרַחֶפֶת עַל־פְּנֵי הַמָּיִם

3 וַיֹּאמֶר אֱלֹהִים יְהִי אוֹר וַיְהִי־אוֹר

4 וַיַּרְא אֱלֹהִים אֶת־הָאוֹר כִּי־טוֹב וַיַּבְדֵּל
אֱלֹהִים בֵּין הָאוֹר וּבֵין הַחֹשֶׁךְ

5 וַיִּקְרָא אֱלֹהִים לָאוֹר יוֹם וְלַחֹשֶׁךְ קָרָא
לָיְלָה וַיְהִי־עֶרֶב וַיְהִי־בֹקֶר יוֹם אֶחָד

6 וַיֹּאמֶר אֱלֹהִים יְהִי רָקִיעַ בְּתוֹךְ הַמָּיִם וִיהִי
מַבְדִּיל בֵּין מַיִם לָמָיִם

7 וַיַּעַשׂ אֱלֹהִים אֶת־הָרָקִיעַ וַיַּבְדֵּל בֵּין הַמַּיִם
אֲשֶׁר מִתַּחַת לָרָקִיעַ וּבֵין הַמַּיִם אֲשֶׁר
מֵעַל לָרָקִיעַ וַיְהִי־כֵן

8 וַיִּקְרָא אֱלֹהִים לָרָקִיעַ שָׁמָיִם וַיְהִי־עֶרֶב
וַיְהִי־בֹקֶר יוֹם שֵׁנִי

9 וַיֹּאמֶר אֱלֹהִים יִקָּווּ הַמַּיִם מִתַּחַת הַשָּׁמַיִם
אֶל־מָקוֹם אֶחָד וְתֵרָאֶה הַיַּבָּשָׁה וַיְהִי־כֵן

10 וַיִּקְרָא אֱלֹהִים לַיַּבָּשָׁה אֶרֶץ וּלְמִקְוֵה הַמַּיִם
קָרָא יַמִּים וַיַּרְא אֱלֹהִים כִּי־טוֹב

11 וַיֹּאמֶר אֱלֹהִים תַּדְשֵׁא הָאָרֶץ דֶּשֶׁא עֵשֶׂב
מַזְרִיעַ זֶרַע עֵץ פְּרִי עֹשֶׂה פְּרִי לְמִינוֹ אֲשֶׁר
זַרְעוֹ־בוֹ עַל־הָאָרֶץ וַיְהִי־כֵן

12 וַתּוֹצֵא הָאָרֶץ דֶּשֶׁא עֵשֶׂב מַזְרִיעַ זֶרַע
לְמִינֵהוּ וְעֵץ עֹשֶׂה־פְּרִי אֲשֶׁר זַרְעוֹ־בוֹ
לְמִינֵהוּ וַיַּרְא אֱלֹהִים כִּי־טוֹב

13 וַיְהִי־עֶרֶב וַיְהִי־בֹקֶר יוֹם שְׁלִישִׁי

14 וַיֹּאמֶר אֱלֹהִים יְהִי מְאֹרֹת בִּרְקִיעַ הַשָּׁמַיִם
לְהַבְדִּיל בֵּין הַיּוֹם וּבֵין הַלָּיְלָה וְהָיוּ לְאֹתֹת
וּלְמוֹעֲדִים וּלְיָמִים וְשָׁנִים

15 וְהָיוּ לִמְאוֹרֹת בִּרְקִיעַ הַשָּׁמַיִם לְהָאִיר עַל־
הָאָרֶץ וַיְהִי־כֵן

16 וַיַּעַשׂ אֱלֹהִים אֶת־שְׁנֵי הַמְּאֹרֹת הַגְּדֹלִים אֶת־
הַמָּאוֹר הַגָּדֹל לְמֶמְשֶׁלֶת הַיּוֹם וְאֶת־הַמָּאוֹר
הַקָּטֹן לְמֶמְשֶׁלֶת הַלַּיְלָה וְאֵת הַכּוֹכָבִים

17 וַיִּתֵּן אֹתָם אֱלֹהִים בִּרְקִיעַ הַשָּׁמָיִם לְהָאִיר
עַל־הָאָרֶץ

18 וְלִמְשֹׁל בַּיּוֹם וּבַלַּיְלָה וּלְהַבְדִּיל בֵּין הָאוֹר
וּבֵין הַחֹשֶׁךְ וַיַּרְא אֱלֹהִים כִּי־טוֹב

19 וַיְהִי־עֶרֶב וַיְהִי־בֹקֶר יוֹם רְבִיעִי

20 וַיֹּאמֶר אֱלֹהִים יִשְׁרְצוּ הַמַּיִם שֶׁרֶץ נֶפֶשׁ חַיָּה
וְעוֹף יְעוֹפֵף עַל־הָאָרֶץ עַל־פְּנֵי רְקִיעַ הַשָּׁמָיִם

21 וַיִּבְרָא אֱלֹהִים אֶת־הַתַּנִּינִם הַגְּדֹלִים וְאֵת כָּל־
נֶפֶשׁ הַחַיָּה הָרֹמֶשֶׂת אֲשֶׁר שָׁרְצוּ הַמַּיִם לְמִינֵהֶם
וְאֵת כָּל־עוֹף כָּנָף לְמִינֵהוּ וַיַּרְא אֱלֹהִים כִּי־טוֹב

22 וַיְבָרֶךְ אֹתָם אֱלֹהִים לֵאמֹר פְּרוּ וּרְבוּ וּמִלְאוּ
אֶת־הַמַּיִם בַּיַּמִּים וְהָעוֹף יִרֶב בָּאָרֶץ

23 וַיְהִי־עֶרֶב וַיְהִי־בֹקֶר יוֹם חֲמִישִׁי

24 וַיֹּאמֶר אֱלֹהִים תּוֹצֵא הָאָרֶץ נֶפֶשׁ חַיָּה לְמִינָהּ
בְּהֵמָה וָרֶמֶשׂ וְחַיְתוֹ־אֶרֶץ לְמִינָהּ וַיְהִי־כֵן

25 וַיַּעַשׂ אֱלֹהִים אֶת־חַיַּת הָאָרֶץ לְמִינָהּ וְאֶת־
הַבְּהֵמָה לְמִינָהּ וְאֵת כָּל־רֶמֶשׂ הָאֲדָמָה לְמִינֵהוּ
וַיַּרְא אֱלֹהִים כִּי־טוֹב

26 וַיֹּאמֶר אֱלֹהִים נַעֲשֶׂה אָדָם בְּצַלְמֵנוּ
כִּדְמוּתֵנוּ וְיִרְדּוּ בִדְגַת הַיָּם וּבְעוֹף הַשָּׁמַיִם
וּבַבְּהֵמָה וּבְכָל־הָאָרֶץ וּבְכָל־הָרֶמֶשׂ הָרֹמֵשׂ
עַל־הָאָרֶץ
27 וַיִּבְרָא אֱלֹהִים אֶת־הָאָדָם בְּצַלְמוֹ בְּצֶלֶם
אֱלֹהִים בָּרָא אֹתוֹ זָכָר וּנְקֵבָה בָּרָא אֹתָם
28 וַיְבָרֶךְ אֹתָם אֱלֹהִים וַיֹּאמֶר לָהֶם אֱלֹהִים
פְּרוּ וּרְבוּ וּמִלְאוּ אֶת־הָאָרֶץ וְכִבְשֻׁהָ וּרְדוּ בִּדְגַת
הַיָּם וּבְעוֹף הַשָּׁמַיִם וּבְכָל־חַיָּה   הָרֹמֶשֶׂת
עַל־הָאָרֶץ
29 וַיֹּאמֶר אֱלֹהִים הִנֵּה נָתַתִּי לָכֶם אֶת־כָּל־עֵשֶׂב
זֹרֵעַ זֶרַע אֲשֶׁר עַל־פְּנֵי כָל־הָאָרֶץ וְאֶת־כָּל־הָעֵץ
אֲשֶׁר־בּוֹ פְרִי־עֵץ זֹרֵעַ זָרַע לָכֶם יִהְיֶה לְאָכְלָה
30 וּלְכָל־חַיַּת הָאָרֶץ וּלְכָל־עוֹף הַשָּׁמַיִם וּלְכֹל
רוֹמֵשׂ עַל־הָאָרֶץ אֲשֶׁר־בּוֹ נֶפֶשׁ חַיָּה אֶת־כָּל־יֶרֶק
עֵשֶׂב לְאָכְלָה וַיְהִי־כֵן
31 וַיַּרְא אֱלֹהִים אֶת־כָּל־אֲשֶׁר עָשָׂה וְהִנֵּה־טוֹב
מְאֹד וַיְהִי־עֶרֶב וַיְהִי־בֹקֶר יוֹם הַשִּׁשִּׁי

Transliteration

1. bey-rey-sheet bah-rah eh-lo-heem eyt hah-shah-mah-yeem veh-eyt hah-ah-rets 2. veh-hah-ah-rets hie-tah tow-huw vah-vow-huw veh-chow-shekh ahl peh-ney teh-howm veh-ruw-ahch eh-low-heem meh-rah-cheh-pheht ahl peh-ney hah-mah-yeem 3. vie-yow-mehr eh-low-heem yeh-hee owr vie-hee owr 4. vie-yahr eh-low-heem eht hah-owr kee towv vie-yahv-deyl eh-low-heem beyn hah-owr uw-veyn hah-chow-shehkh 5. vie-yeeq-rah eh-low-heem lah-owr yowm veh-lah-chow-shehkh qah-rah lie-lah vie-hee eh-rehv vie-hee vow-qehr yowm eh-chahd 6. vie-yow-mehr eh-low-heem yeh-hee rah-qee-ah beh-towkh hah-mah-yeem vee-hee mahv-deel beyn mah-yeem lah-mah-yeem 7. vie-yah-ahs eh-low-heem eht hah-rah-qee-ah vie-yahv-deyl beyn hah-mah-yeem ah-shehr mee-tah-chaht lah-rah-qee-ah uw-veyn hah-mah-yeem ah-shehr mey-ahl lah-rah-qee-ah vie-hee kheyn 8. vie-yeeq-rah eh-low-heem lah-rah-qee-ah shah-mah-yeem vie-hee eh-rehv vie-hee vow-qehr yowm shey-nee 9. vie-yow-mehr eh-low-heem yee-qahv-vuw hah-mah-yeem mee-tah-chaht hah-shah-mah-yeem ehl mah-qowm eh-chahd veh-tey-rah-eh hie-yah-bah-shah vie-hee kheyn 10. vie-yeeq-rah eh-low-heem lie-yah-bah-shah eh-rehts uwl-meeq-vey hah-mah-yeem qah-rah yahm-meem vie-yahr eh-low-heem kee towv 11. vie-yow-mehr eh-low-heem tahd-shey hah-ah-rehts deh-sheh ey-sehv mahz-ree-ah zeh-rah eyts peh-ree ow-seh peh-ree leh-mee-now ah-shehr zahr-ow vow ahl hah-ah-rets vie-hee kheyn 12. vah-tow-tsey hah-ah-rehts deh-sheh ey-sehv mahz-ree-ah zeh-rah leh-mee-ney-huw veh-eyts ow-seh peh-ree ah-shehr zahr-ow vow leh-mee-ney-huw vie-yahr eh-low-heem kee tow 13. vie-hee eh-rehv vie-hee vow-qehr yowm sheh-lee-shee 14.

vie-yow-mehr eh-low-heem yeh-hee meh-ow-rowt beer-
qee-ah hah-shah-mah-yeem leh-hahv-deel beyn hah-
yowm uw-veyn hah-lie-lah veh-hie-uw leh-owt-owt uwl-
mow-ah-deem uwl-yah-meem veh-shah-neem 15. veh-
hie-uw leem-ow-rowt beer-qee-ah hah-shah-mah-yeem
leh-hah-eer ahl hah-ah-rets vie-hee kheyn 16. vie-yah-ahs
eh-low-heem eht sheh-ney hah-meh-ow-rowt hahg-dow-
leem eht hah-mah-owr hah-gah-dowl leh-mehm-sheh-leht
hah-yowm veh-eht hah-mah-owr hah-qah-town   leh-
mehm-sheh-leht hah-lie-lah veh-eyt hah-kow-khah-veem
17. vie-yee-teyn ow-tahm eh-low-heem beer-qee-ah hah-
shah-mah-yeem leh-hah-eer ahl hah-ah-rehts 18. veh-
leem-showl bah-yowm uw-vah-lie-lah uw-lah-hahv-deel
beyn hah-owr uw-veyn hah-chow-shehkh vie-yahr eh-
low-heem kee towv 19. vie-hee eh-rehv vie-hee vow-qehr
yowm reh-vee-ee 20. vie-yow-mehr eh-low-heem yeesh-
reh-tsuw hah-mah-yeem sheh-rehts neh-phehsh hie-yah
veh-uwph yeh-ow-pheyph ahl hah-ah-rehts ahl peh-ney
reh-qee-ah hah-shah-mah-yeem 21. vie-yeev-rah eh-low-
heem eht hah-tah-nee-neem hahg-dow-leem veh-eyt kowl
neh-phehsh hah-chie-yah hah-row-meh-sheht ah-shehr
shahr-tsuw hah-mah-yeem leh-mee-ney-hehm veh-eyt
kowl owph kah-nahph leh-mee-ney-huw vie-yahr eh-low-
heem kee towv 22. vie-vah-rekh ow-tahm eh-low-heem
ley-mowr peh-ruw uwr-vuw uw-meel-uw eht hah-mah-
yeem bah-yah-meem veh-hah-owph yee-rehv bah-ah-
rehts 23. vie-hee eh-rehv vie-hee vow-qehr yowm chah-
mee-shee 24. vie-yow-mehr eh-low-heem tow-tsey hah-
ah-rehts neh-phehsh chie-yah leh-mee-nah beh-hey-mah
vah-reh-mehs veh-chie-tow eh-rehts leh-mee-nah vie-hee
kheyn 25. vie-yah-ahs eh-low-heem eht chie-yaht hah-ah-
rets leh-mee-nah veh-eht hah-beh-hey-mah leh-mee-nah
veh-eyt kowl reh-mehs hah-ah-dah-mah leh-mee-ney-huw
vie-yahr eh-low-heem kee towv 26. vie-yow-mehr eh-
low-heem nah-ah-seh ah-dahm beh-tsahl-mey-nuw keed-

muw-tey-nuw veh-yeer-duw veed-gaht hah-yahm uwv-owph hah-shah-mah-yeem uw-vah-beh-hey-mah uwv-khowl hah-ah-rehts uwv-khowl hah-reh-mehs hah-row-meys ahl hah-ah-rets 27. vie-yeev-rah eh-low-heem eht hah-ah-dahm beh-tsahl-mow beh-tseh-lehm eh-low-heem bah-rah ow-tow zah-khahr uw-neh-qey-vah bah-rah ow-tahm 28. vie-vah-rehkh ow-tahm eh-low-heem vie-yow-mehr lah-hehm eh-low-heem peh-ruw uwr-vuw uw-meel-uw eht hah-ah-rehts veh-kheev-shuw-ah uwr-duw beed-gaht hah-yahm uwv-owph hah-shah-mah-yeem uwv-khowl chie-yah hah-row-meh-seht ahl hah-ah-rehts 29. vie-yow-mehr eh-low-heem heen-ney nah-tah-tee lah-khehm eht kowl ey-sehv zow-rey-ah zeh-rah ah-shehr ahl peh-ney khowl hah-ah-rehts veh-eht kowl hah-eyts ah-shehr bow peh-ree eyts zow-rey-ah zah-rah lah-khehm yee-yeh leh-ahkh-lah 30. uwl-khowl chie-yaht hah-ah-rehts uwl-khowl owph hah-shah-mah-yeem uwl-khowl row-meys ahl hah-ah-rehts ah-shehr bow neh-phehsh chie-yah eht kowl yeh-rehq ey-sehv leh-ahkh-lah vie-hee kheyn 31. vie-yahr eh-low-heem eht kowl ah-shehr ah-sah veh-heen-ney towv meh-owd vie-hee eh-rehv vie-hee vow-qehr yowm hah-shee-shee

Part 3
Reference Guide

The purpose of the Reference Guide is to be an aid to the Hebrew student to assist with recognzing the prefixes and suffixes of Hebrew nouns and verbs.

Uncovering the root word

One Hebrew word may contain a root, one or two prefixes as well as one or two suffixes. As an example, let us look at the word וַיְדַבֵּר‎ם. To find the root word, we first identify the prefixes and suffixes. The prefix ו means "and." The י is another prefix identifying the subject of the verb as a "he." The suffix ם identifies the object of the verb as "them." Once the suffix and prefixes are removed we have the root דבר, meaning "speak," remaining. The Hebrew word וַיְדַבֵּר‎ם, means "and he spoke to them."

53

Identification of the prefixes and suffixes of a verb will assist you in translating each word correctly. This will also allow you to uncover the root of the word, which can then be looked up in the root dictionary below.

Prefixes - The article, conjunction and prepositions

Some of the most common words found in the Bible are actually written as prefixes, such as ב (in), ו (and), ה (the) and ל (to). The two prefixes כ (like) and ש (which) are also used but occur infrequently. Combining a prefix with a suffix also forms words. For example, the word לך is the prefix ל meaning "to" and the suffix ך meaning "you" (see possessive pronouns below) forming a word meaning "to you."

Prefixes			
The	הָ--	And	ו--
To	ל--	In	בְ--
From	מִ--	Like	כְ--
Which, who	שְׁ--		

Plural

Nouns are made plural by adding the following suffixes. There are a few exceptions to these gender specific suffixes. For example אב (father) and אור (light) are masculine words yet carry the feminine suffix, אבות and אורות, but still remain masculine.

Plural Suffixes	
Masculine	**Feminine**
‑‑ים	‑‑ות

Noun derivatives

Included in this section is a list of the most common prefixes, infixes and suffixes added to a root to form a new noun. Each noun derivitive will be related in meaning to the original root word. By recognizing these "fixes," one can easily uncover the original root word assisting the reader with identifying the meaning of the word. For example, the words צדיק and צדקה are derived from the root צדק (righteous). The word צדיק is formed by infixing the letter י and has the meaning of "a righteous one." The word צדקה is formed by suffixing the letter ה and has the meaning of "righteousness."

Noun Derivitives		
‑‑מ	‑‑מ‑‑	‑‑י‑‑
‑‑ת	‑‑ת‑‑	‑‑ִי‑‑
‑‑ה	‑‑ות‑‑	‑‑וֹן
	‑‑ית‑‑	

Pronouns

The following pronouns are very common and a good understanding of them will assist the student in reading the text.

Pronouns			
Singular		**Plural**	
Masculine			
I	אֲנִי	We	אֲנוּ
You	אַתָּה	You	אַתֶּם
He	הוּא	They	הֵם
Feminine			
I	אֲנִי	We	אֲנוּ
You	אַתְּ	You	אַתֵּן
She	הִיא	They	הֵן

Possessive Pronouns (Nouns)			
Singular		**Plural**	
Masculine			
My	‐‐ִי	Our	‐‐נוּ
Your	‐‐ְךָ	Your	‐‐ְכֶם
His	‐‐וֹ	Their	‐‐ָם
Feminine			
My	‐‐ִי	Our	‐‐נוּ
Your	‐‐ֵךְ	Your	‐‐ְכֶן
Her	‐‐ָהּ	Their	‐‐ֶן

Hebrew Tenses

Hebrew verb tenses are not related to time (past, present or future), as in English, but to action. There are two Hebrew tenses, perfect and imperfect. The perfect tense is complete action and is similar to past tense. The imperfect tense is incomplete action (action that has started but not finished or action that has not started) and is similar to our present and future tense.

Each verb will also identify the person, gender and number of the subject of the verb. The person is expressed as first, second or third person, the gender will be either masculine or feminine and the number will be singular or plural.

Using the Hebrew root word שמר (to guard), the letter א is prefixed to form the verb אשמר. The addition of this letter indicates that the verb is first person, masculine, singular and imperfect tense - "I am guarding" or "I will guard." By suffixing the letters תִי, the verb שָׁמַרְתִּי is formed, and is first person, masculine, singular, perfect tense - "I guarded."

When the conjuction ו (meaning "and") is prefixed to a verb, the tense is reversed. While אֶשְׁמֹר means "I will guard" (imperfect tense), וָאֶשְׁמֹר becomes "I guarded" (perfect tense). While שָׁמַרְתִּי means "I gaurded" (perfect tense), וְשָׁמַרְתִּי becomes "I will guard" (imperfect tense).

Verb Subjects (Perfect Tense)			
Singular		**Plural**	
Masculine			
I	־־תִּי	We	־־נוּ
You	־־תָ	You	־־תֶּם
He	־־	They	־־וּ
Feminine			
I	־־י	We	־־נוּ
You	־־תְּ	You	־־תֶּן
She	־־ָה	They	־־וּ

Verb Subjects (Imperfect Tense)			
Singular		**Plural**	
Masculine			
I	אֶ־־	We	נ־־
You	תִּ־־	You	תִּ־־וּ
He	יִ־־	They	יִ־־וּ
Feminine			
I	אֶ־־	We	נ־־
You	תִּ־־י	You	תִּ־־נָה
She	תִּ־־	They	תִּ־־נָה

Part 4
Translating Lessons

Your next step in Biblical Hebrew studies is to learn sentence and word structure. The following is the first five verses of Genesis chapter one where we will examine each word, one at a time, explaining their construction and relationship within the sentence. These lessons will frequently refer to prefixes, suffixes and roots that can be found in Referene Guide of this book.

Lesson 1 – Genesis 1:1

בְּרֵאשִׁית בָּרָא אֱלֹהִים אֵת הַשָּׁמַיִם וְאֵת הָאָרֶץ

בראשית

The בּ is a prefix meaning "inside" or "in." This letter is an abbreviated form of the Hebrew word בַּיִת (beyt) meaning, "house." Inside the house is where the family resides. (For a list of the common prefixes see the chart labeled "Prefixes" in Part 3)

The root word is ראשׁ (rosh) meaning, "head." Adding certain letters to the root commonly forms words related in meaning to the root and all of the words derived from the same root will be related in meaning. In this case, the letters ית are added to the root to form a noun, ראשׁית. This word means "beginning," the head of a time or space as in the beginning of an event or a river. (For a list of common letters used to form new nouns, see the chart labeled "Noun Derivatives" in Part 3)

By being able to recognize the letters added to a root to form noun derivatives, one can easily find the root within the word. There are approximately 8,000 different words in the Hebrew Bible, all of which are derived from only about 1,500 roots. Of these 1,500, about half are rarely used in the Bible. This means that with a good understanding of about 750 roots one can easily read the

Biblical text without memorizing all 8,000 words used within it.

בְּרָא

This is a verb usually translated as "create."

Each verb identifies person (first, second or third), gender (masculine or feminine), number (singular or plural) and tense (perfect or imperfect). This verb would be literally translated as "he created." The construction of the verb identifies the subject of the verb as third person, masculine, singular and perfect tense. (For the various prefixes and suffixes added to the verb to identify person, gender, number and tense, see the verb charts in Part 3)

Perfect tense is completed action and is similar to our past tense. Imperfect tense is incomplete action and is similar to our present or future tense. Notice the difference of tenses between Hebrew and English. English tenses are related to time (past, present or future) while Hebrew is related to action (complete or incomplete).

אֱלֹהִים

This word is the subject of the verb, the "he" in "he created." Generally the subject of the verb will follow the verb rather than precede it as in English. In English we say "God created" but in Hebrew this would be written as "created God."

The root word for this noun is אֵלָה meaning "power." This word is used for anyone or anything which, has "power" and is often translated as "God." The suffix ‎‏םי‏‎ denotes a plural for masculine nouns. While English plurals convey quantity (more than one), Hebrew plurals convey quantity or quality (very large or great). The word ‎‏אלהים‏‎ can be translated as "gods" (quantity) or "a great god" (quality). The idea of "a great god" is generally written in English as "God."

Only through context can it be determined if the plural noun is identifying quantity or quality. This can be the context within the passage or the sentence structure itself. In this verse the context of the sentence structure requires this word to be understood as qualitative since the verb preceding it states "he (singular) created" and not "they (plural) created."

‎‏את‏‎

This word ‎‏את‏‎ is used over 11,000 times (and never translated into English as there is no equivalent) to point to the direct object of the verb. Some examples of a direct object are "Bible," "the book" and "his book" where the "book" is specifically identified." Conversely, an example of an indirect object would be "a book" where the book is not specifically identified.

השמים

The first letter, ה, is another prefix and is usually translated as "the" (definite article). This prefix is the short form of the word הל meaning, "to look at something."

The root word is שׁמים meaning, "sky" or "heaven." Several Hebrew words are always written in the plural form such as this word.

Because the ה (the) precedes the word שׁמים, this word is a direct object of the verb ברא, hence, the reason for the word את before it.

ואת

Another very common prefix is the letter ו, usually translated as "and." This is the abbreviated form of the word וו meaning, peg or nail. As a nail attaches two items together, this prefix attaches two or more things together in a sentence, in this case "the skies and the land."

Added to this prefix is the word את which was previously discussed. Because of this word we know that the word which follows is also a direct object of the verb ברא.

הָאָרֶץ

The letter הַ is the prefix meaning "the." The word אֶרֶץ is a common word meaning, "land" or "earth."

Learn to Read Biblical Hebrew

Lesson 2 – Genesis 1:2

וְהָאָרֶץ הָיְתָה תֹהוּ וָבֹהוּ וְחֹשֶׁךְ עַל־פְּנֵי תְהוֹם
תְהוֹם וְרוּחַ אֱלֹהִים מְרַחֶפֶת עַל־פְּנֵי הַמָּיִם

וְהָאָרֶץ

As previously discussed the prefix וֹ is used to attach two parts of a sentence together but is also used to attach two or more sentences together, in other words bringing all of the words of one story together. In fact, the entire chapter of Genesis chapter one is one long story as each sentence begins with a וֹ.

The letter הָ is the prefix meaning "the" and the word אֶרֶץ, as previously discussed, means "land."

הָיְתָה

The root of this verb is הָיָה, a very common root literally meaning, "to exist" or "breath" as one who exists breaths but is usually translated with a form of the English verb "to be." This verb is made feminine, singular, and perfect tense by adding the הָ to the end of the root (הָיָהה). When a הָ is added as a suffix to a root that ends with a הָ, this הָ is changed to a תָ (הָיָתָה). This verb would be literally translated as "she existed" where the "she" is the "land," the previous word.

תהו

The root word here is תה meaning "empty." By adding the suffix letter ו to the root, a noun derivative is formed meaning, "empty" or "void."

ובהו

The first letter, ו, is the prefix meaning "and" and is used to connect this word with the previous word.

The root word is בה meaning, "to fill a void." A common Hebrew word also derived from this root is בוא (bo') and is usually translated as "come" or "go." The English translations of this word imply movement in a certain direction but the Hebrew meaning of the word בוא is to "fill a void" and can be either fill a void here (come) or fill a void there (go).

The ו added after the root forms a noun derivative meaning, "void."

The phrase תהו ובהו is a common style of poetry where similar sounding words are grouped together. While the phrase "The painter painted a painting with paint," would be poor English, it is a perfect example of Hebrew poetry.

וְחֹשֶׁךְ

The first letter is the prefix וֹ, meaning "and." The word חֹשֶׁךְ means "dark" or "darkness."

עַל

This word is very common and means "over" or "on."

פְּנֵי

The root for this word is פָּנָה meaning, face. This word is always used in the plural form פָּנִים (the ה is dropped when the masculine plural suffix is added). This word is in the construct state "faces of....."

When a masculine plural noun is used in the Construct State, the letter ם is always dropped.

תְהוֹם

A noun derived from the root הוֹם meaning "sea," closely related in form to the more common word for sea, יָם. This noun derivative is formed by adding the prefix letter ת, and has the more specific meaning of "deep sea." This and the previous word form the Construct phrase "faces of the deep."

ורוח

The first letter **ו** is the prefix meaning "and." The word **רוח** is another Hebrew word meaning, "wind." Though this word is often translated as "spirit" the more Hebraic understanding is "wind" or "breath."

אלהים

This is the same word discussed previously. When two nouns appear together they are in the Construct State. This word and the preceding word, **רוח**, would be translated as "wind/breath of God."

מרחפת

The root to this verb is **רחף** meaning, "hover over" such as a bird does over the nest. The letter **מ** is a prefix added to the verb to form a conjugation. The letter **ת** indicates this verb is feminine singular perfect tense and literally translated as "she hovered." The "she" of this word is the previous word **רוח**, a feminine word. While most consider the "Spirit" (wind/breath) a "he," Biblically, it is a "she."

על

This is the same word previously discussed meaning "over" or "on."

פְּנֵי

This word was also previously discussed meaning "faces" and is in the construct state with the following word.

הַמִּים

The first letter הַ is the prefix meaning "the." The root word is מִים, a very common word meaning, "water."

Notice that the previous sentence contains no verb. While a verb is required in every English sentence it is not in Biblical Hebrew.

Learn to Read Biblical Hebrew

Lesson 3 – Genesis 1:3

וַיֹּאמֶר אֱלֹהִים יְהִי אוֹר וַיְהִי־אוֹר

וַיֹּאמֶר

The first letter וֹ is the prefix meaning "and." The root word is אָמַר.

Hebrew root words can be used as a noun or a verb. As a noun this root would mean a "word" while as a verb it means, "to say." We see a similar occurrence in English as in the sentence; "He will play Moses in the play." The first use of the word "play" is a verb while the second is a noun. The context of the sentence as well as the type of prefixes and suffixes added to the word will tell you if the word is a verb or a noun.

When the letter ' is added to the root אָמַר, the word is identified as a verb and can literally be translated as "he says" or "he will say" (masculine, singular, perfect tense).

When the letter vav is prefixed to a verb, the tense of the verb is reversed. Therefore, the word יֹאמַר is "he says" (masculine, singular, imperfect tense) while the word וַיֹּאמֶר is "he said" (masculine, singular, perfect tense). This vav, when used in this instance, is called the "vav consecutive."

אֱלֹהִים

This word has been discussed previously and is the subject of the previous verb.

יְהִי

The root of this word is הָיָה as discussed previously meaning, "to exist." When the letter י is prefixed to the root, the word יִהְיֶה (masculine, singular, imperfect tense) is formed, meaning, "he exists."

When a root ends with a ה, it is often dropped when used as a verb. Hence, יִהְיֶה becomes יְהִי. Another letter that frequently drops off a root when used as a verb is the letter נ when it is the first letter of the root. All verb roots consist of three letters. If you come across a verb and remove the prefixes and suffixes and find only two letters remaining, most likely the verb has dropped the final ה or the beginning נ. For example, in Genesis 17:3 we find the word וַיִּפֹּל. The letter ו is the vav consecutive meaning "and" and reverses the tense of the verb. The letter י is the prefix identifying the subject of the verb as masculine singular. We are then left with the word פֹּל. The missing third letter for this root is the dropped נ as the root is נָפֹל.

אוֹר

This is a root word meaning "light." This word is the subject of the previous verb.

וַיְהִי

This is the same verb with the same conjugation as the previous verb but includes the וֹ, which reverses the tense from imperfect to perfect, and becomes "and he existed."

אוֹר

The same word meaning, light, and again, the subject of the previous verb.

Lesson 4 – Genesis 1:4 & 5

וַיַּרְא אֱלֹהִים אֶת־הָאוֹר כִּי־טוֹב וַיַּבְדֵּל
אֱלֹהִים בֵּין הָאוֹר וּבֵין הַחֹשֶׁךְ
וַיִּקְרָא אֱלֹהִים לָאוֹר יוֹם וְלַחֹשֶׁךְ קָרָא
לַיְלָה וַיְהִי־עֶרֶב וַיְהִי־בֹקֶר יוֹם אֶחָד

At this point you should be able to translate verses 4 and 5. Most of the words as well as the prefixes and suffixes have been covered above with the exception of those listed below. Once you have translated the verses you can use your English Bible to check your translation.

To see	ראה		To call	קרא
To separate	בדל		Good	טוב
Between	בין		That, it is	כי
Night	לילה		Day	יום
Evening	ערב		Morning	בקר
One	אחד		To (prefix)	ל

Learn to Read Biblical Hebrew

Part 5
Hebrew/English
Dictionary

This list contains all the words used in the Bible which occur twenty-five times or more. For example, the word ראשון (used 182 times) is derived from the root ראש (used 615 times), both being included in the list. The word ראשית (used 1 time) is also derived from the same root, but is used less than twenty-five times in the Bible and is not included in the dictionary.

The Hebrew words in this dictionary do not contain any of the prefixes or suffixes as found in the Hebrew text. By removing the prefixes and suffixes of the Hebrew words in the text, the word can be found. For example the word השמים, includes the prefix ה meaning "the." When this is removed, the word שמים, meaning "heavens," remains and is found in the dictionary. As another example, the word ויאמרו, meaning "and they said," contains two prefixes (ו and י), and one suffix (ו). When these are removed, the word אמר meaning "to say," remains and is also found in the dictionary.

English	Hebrew	English	Hebrew
Father	אָב	Brother	אָח
To destroy	אָבַד	One	אֶחָד
Consent	אָבָה	Back, Future	אָחוֹר
Needy	אֶבְיוֹן	Sister	אָחוֹת
To mourn	אָבַל	To seize	אָחַז
Stone	אֶבֶן	Possession	אֲחֻזָּה
Lord	אָדוֹן	After	אַחַר
Nobles	אַדִּיר	Other	אַחֵר
Mankind	אָדָם	Last	אַחֲרוֹן
Ground	אֲדָמָה	Future	אַחֲרִית
Base	אֶדֶן	Where	אֵי
Lord	אֲדֹנָי	Island	אִי
To love	אָהַב	Enemy	אֹיֵב
Love	אַהֲבָה	Where	אַיֵּה
Tent	אֹהֶל	How	אֵיךְ
Or	אוֹ	Ram	אַיִל
Desire	אַוָּה	Arch	אֵילָם
Fool	אֱוִיל	Not exist	אַיִן
Perhaps	אוּלַי	Man	אִישׁ
Folly	אִוֶּלֶת	But	אַךְ
Evil	אָוֶן	To eat	אָכַל
Wheel	אוֹפָן	Food	אֹכֶל
Treasure	אוֹצָר	Not	אַל
To Shine	אוֹר	God	אֵל
Light	אוֹר	To	אֶל
Sign	אוֹת	Oath	אָלָה
Then	אָז	These	אֵלֶּה
To Listen	אָזַן	God(s)	אֱלֹהִים
Ear	אֹזֶן	God	אֱלוֹהַּ

English	Hebrew	English	Hebrew

Learn to Read Biblical Hebrew

English	Hebrew	English	Hebrew
Chief	אַלּוּף	Four	אַרְבַּע
Widow	אַלְמָנָה	Forty	אַרְבָּעִים
Thousand	אֶלֶף	Purple	אַרְגָּמָן
Mother	אֵם	Chest	אָדוֹן
If	אִם	Cedar	אֶרֶז
Maidservant	אָמָה	Path	אֹרַח
Cubit	אַמָּה	Lion	אֲרִי
Faithfulness	אֱמוּנָה	To lengthen	אָרַךְ
To believe	אָמַן	Length	אֹרֶךְ
Amen	אָמֵן	Fortress	אַדְמוֹן
Courageous	אַמֵּץ	Earth, land	אֶרֶץ
To say	אָמַר	To curse	אָרַר
Word	אֵמֶר	Fire	אֵשׁ
Promise	אִמְרָה	Off. by fire	אִשֶּׁה
Truth, faith	אֱמֶת	Woman	אִשָּׁה
Where	אָן	To bear guilt	אָשֵׁם
Man	אֱנוֹשׁ	Guilt (off.)	אָשָׁם
We	אֲנַחְנוּ	Which	אֲשֶׁר
I	אֲנִי	Blessed	אַשְׁרֵי
Ship	אֳנִיָּה	[with]	אֵת
I	אָנֹכִי	You	אַתָּה
To gather	אָסַף	Donkey (f)	אָתוֹן
To bind	אָסַר	Well	בְּאֵר
And	אַף	To be unfaithful	בָּגַד
Nose, anger	אַף	Clothes	בֶּגֶד
End	אֶפֶס	Pole, alone	בַּד
Finger	אֶצְבַּע	To set apart	בָּדַל
Beside	אֵצֶל	To terrify	בָּהַל
To ambush	אָרַב	Animal	בְּהֵמָה

English	Hebrew	English	Hebrew
To come	בּוֹא	Master	בַּעַל

81

Learn to Read Biblical Hebrew

Pit	בּוֹר	To burn	בָּעַר
To disgrace	בּוֹשׁ	To fortify	בָּצַר
Plunder	בַּז	To divide	בָּקַע
Despise	בָּזָה	Herd	בָּקָר
To carry off	בָּזַז	Morning	בֹּקֶר
Young man	בָּחוּר	To seek	בָּקַשׁ
To test	בָּחַן	To create	בָּרָא
To choose	בָּחַר	Hail	בָּרָד
To trust	בָּטַח	Iron	בַּרְזֶל
Safety	בֶּטַח	To flee	בָּרַח
Womb	בֶּטֶן	Bar	בְּרִיחַ
To understand	בִּין	Covenant	בְּרִית
Between	בֵּין	To bless	בָּרַךְ
Understanding	בִּינָה	Knee	בֶּרֶךְ
House	בַּיִת	Blessing	בְּרָכָה
To weep	בָּכָה	To cook	בָּשַׁל
Firstborn	בְּכֹר	Spice	בֹּשֶׂם
Weep	בְּכִי	Flesh	בָּשָׂר
Not, less	בַּל	Shame	בֹּשֶׁת
Not, Without	בְּלִי	Daughter	בַּת
Wicked	בְּלִיַּעַל	Virgin	בְּהוּלָה
To mix	בָּלַל	Pride	גָּאוֹן
To swallow	בָּלַע	To redeem	גָּאַל
Not, Without	בִּלְתִּי	To make high	גָּבַח
High place	בָּמָה	High	גָּבַה
Son	בֵּן	Territory	גְּבוּל
To build	בָּנָה	Mighty	גִּבּוֹר
For	בַּעַד	Power	גְּבוּרָה

Learn to Read Biblical Hebrew

English	Hebrew	English	Hebrew
Hill	גִּבְעָה	Plague	דֶּבֶר
To strengthen	גָּבַר	Honey	דְּבַשׁ
Strong man	גֶּבֶר	Grain	דָּגָן
Roof	גָּג	Uncle	דּוֹד
Troops	גְּדוּד	Generation	דּוֹר
Great	גָּדוֹל	Enough	דַּי
To make great	גָּדַל	Poor	דַּל
Nation	גּוֹי	Door	דֶּלֶת
Exile	גּוֹלָה	Blood	דָּם
To be alien	גּוּר	To compare	דָּמָה
Lot	גּוֹרָל	Likeness	דְּמוּת
To rob	גָּזַל	Knowledge	דַּעַת
Valley	גַּיְא	To tread	דָּרַךְ
To rejoice	גִּיל	Way	דֶּרֶךְ
To exile	גָּלָה	To seek	דָּרַשׁ
Idols	גִּלּוּל	Meaningless	הֶבֶל
Also	גַּם	To mutter	הָגָה
To wean	גָּמַל	Splendor	הָדָר
Camel	גָּמָל	He	הוּא
Garden	גַּן	Woe	הוֹי
To steal	גָּנַב	Wealth	הוֹן
Vine	גֶּפֶן	To exist	הָיָה
Alien	גֵּר	Temple	הֵיכָל
Threshing floor	גֹּרֶן	To go/walk	הָלַךְ
To drive out	גָּרַשׁ	To praise	הָלַל
Rain	גֶּשֶׁם	They	הֵם
To cling	דָּבַק	To roar	הָמָה
To speak	דָּבַר	Crowd	הָמוֹן
Word	דָּבָר	Surely	הֵן

Learn to Read Biblical Hebrew

English	Hebrew	English	Hebrew
Here	הֵנָּה	Feast	חַג
Look	הִנֵּה	To put on	חָגַר
To turn	הָפַךְ	To stop	חָדַל
Mountain	הַר	Bedroom	חֶדֶר
To kill	הָרַג	New	חָדָשׁ
To conceive	הָרָה	New moon	חֹדֶשׁ
To tear down	הָרַס	To anguish	חוּל
To sacrifice	זָבַח	Wall	חוֹמָה
Sacrifice	זֶבַח	Street	חוּץ
This	זֶה	To see	חָזָה
Gold	זָהָב	Vision	חָזוֹן
To flow	זוּב	To strengthen	חָזַק
Olive	זַיִת	Strong	חָזָק
To remember	זָכַר	To sin	חָטָא
Male	זָכָר	Sin	חֵטְא
Lewdness	זִמָּה	Sin (off.)	חַטָּאת
To make music	זָמַר	Wheat	חִטָּה
To prostitute	זָנָה	Life	חַי
To cry out	זָעַק	To live	חָיָה
Old, elder	זָקֵן	Army	חַיִל
To scatter	זָרָה	Outer	חִיצוֹן
Arm	זְרוֹעַ	Bosom	חֵיק
To plant	זָרַע	To be wise	חָכַם
Seed	זֶרַע	Wise	חָכָם
To sprinkle	זָרַק	Wisdom	חָכְמָה
To hide	חָבָא	Fat	חֵלֶב
Rope	חֶבֶל	Milk	חָלָב
To join	חָבַר	To be ill	חָלָה
To saddle	חָבַשׁ	Dream	חֲלוֹם

84

Learn to Read Biblical Hebrew

English	Hebrew	English	Hebrew
Window	חַלּוֹן	To search	חָקַר
To begin	חָלַל	To lay waste	חָרַב
Slain	חָלָל	Sword	חֶרֶב
To dream	חָלַם	Ruins	חָרְבָּה
To change	חָלַף	To tremble	חָרַד
To divide	חָלַק	Anger	חָרָה
Portion	חֵלֶק	Fierce	חָרוֹן
Wrath	חֵמָה	To destroy	חָרַם
Donkey (m)	חֲמוֹר	Destroy	חֵרֶם
Fifth	חֲמִישִׁי	To insult	חָרַף
To spare	חָמַל	Disgrace	חֶרְפָּה
Violence	חָמָס	To plow	חָרַשׁ
Five	חָמֵשׁ	Craftsman	חָרָשׁ
Grace	חֵן	To plan	חָשַׁב
To camp	חָנָה	To hold back	חָשַׂךְ
Spear	חֲנִית	Darkness	חֹשֶׁךְ
For no reason	חִנָּם	Breastpiece	חֹשֶׁן
To have grace	חָנַן	To seal	חָתַם
Love	חֶסֶד	To frighten	חָתַת
To take refuge	חָסָה	Guard	טַבָּח
Saints	חָסִיד	Ring	טַבַּעַת
Delight	חֵפֶץ	Pure	טָהוֹר
Delight	חֵפֶץ	To be pure	טָהֵר
Arrow	חֵץ	Good	טוֹב
half	חֲצִי	Goodness	טוּב
Trumpet	חֲצֹצְרָה	Good	טוֹבָה
Courtyard	חָצֵר	Row	טוּר
Decree	חֹק	Dew	טַל
Decree	חֻקָּה	To be unclean	טָמֵא

Learn to Read Biblical Hebrew

English	Hebrew	English	Hebrew
Unclean	טָמֵא	To discipline	יִסַּר
Uncleanness	טֻמְאָה	To meet	יָעַד
To hide	טָמַן	Because	יַעַן
Children	טַף	To give advise	יָעַץ
Before	טֶרֶם	Forest	יַעַר
To tear	טָרַף	Beautiful	יָפֶה
To dry up	יָבֵשׁ	To come out	יָצָה
To be weary	יָגַע	To stand	יָצַב
Hand	יָד	To pour out	יָצַק
To throw	יָדָה	To form	יָצַר
To know	יָדַע	To set fire	יָצַת
Day	יוֹם	Precious	יָקָר
Day	יוֹמָם	To fear	יָרֵא
Dove	יוֹנָה	Fear	יִרְאָה
Together	יַחַד	To come down	יָרַד
Together	יַחְדּוּ	To shoot	יָרָה
To hope	יָחַל	Moon	יָרֵחַ
To do good	יָטַב	Curtain	יְרִיעָה
Wine	יַיִן	Side	יָרֵךְ
To rebuke	יָכַח	Far, end	יְרֵכָה
Could	יָכֹל	To take possession	יָרַשׁ
To bear child	יָלַד	There is	יֵשׁ
Child	יֶלֶד	To settle	יָשַׁב
To wail	יָלַל	Salvation	יְשׁוּעָה
Sea, West	יָם	To save	יָשַׁע
Right	יָמִין	Salvation	יֵשַׁע
Right	יְמָנִי	To straighten	יָשַׁר
To lay found.	יָסַד	Upright	יָשָׁר
To add	יָסַף	Peg	יָתֵד

86

Learn to Read Biblical Hebrew

English	Hebrew	English	Hebrew
Fatherless	יָתוֹם	Harp	כִּנּוֹר
To be left	יָתַר	To humble	כָּנַע
Other	יֶתֶר	Wing, Corner	כָּנָף
Heavy	כָּבֵד	Throne	כִּסֵּא
Glory	כָּבוֹד	To cover	כָּסָה
To wash	כָּבַס	Fool	כְּסִיל
Lamb (m)	כֶּבֶשׂ	Silver	כֶּסֶף
This is what	כֹּה	To mk angry	כָּעַס
Priest	כֹּהֵן	Palm, Sole	כַּף
Star	כּוֹכָב	Young lion	כְּפִיר
To hold	כּוּל	To atone	כָּפַר
To prepare	כּוּן	Mercy seat	כַּפֹּרֶת
Cup	כּוֹס	Vineyard	כֶּרֶם
To lie	כָּזַב	To bow down	כָּרַע
Strength	כֹּחַ	To cut off	כָּרַת
To hide	כָּחַד	To stumble	כָּשַׁל
For	כִּי	To write	כָּתַב
This is how	כָּכָה	Robe	כֻּתֹּנֶת
Talent, plain	כִּכָּר	Side	כָּתֵף
All	כֹּל	No, Not	לֹא
Dog	כֶּלֶב	People	לְאֹם
To finish	כָּלָה	Heart	לֵב
Daughter in-law	כַּלָּה	Heart	לֵבָב
Article	כְּלִי	Clothing	לְבוּשׁ
Kidney	כִּלְיָה	White	לָבָן
To disgrace	כָּלַם	To clothe	לָבַשׁ
Disgrace	כְּלִמָּה	If	לוּ
Like	כְּמוֹ	Tablet	לוּחַ
So	כֵּן	To stay a night	לוּן

Learn to Read Biblical Hebrew

English	Hebrew	English	Hebrew
To fight	לָחַם	To circumcise	מוּל
Bread	לֶחֶם	Near	מוּל
Night	לַיְלָה	To discipline	מוּסָר
To catch	לָכַד	Meeting	מוֹעֵד
To learn	לָמַד	Wonders	מוֹפֵת
To take	לָקַח	Exit	מוֹצָה
To gather	לָקַט	Snare	מוֹקֵשׁ
Tongue	לָשׁוֹן	Settlement	מוֹשָׁב
Room	לִשְׁכָּה	To die	מוּת
Very	מְאֹד	Death	מָוֶת
Hundred	מֵאָה	Altar	מִזְבֵּחַ
Anything	מְאוּמָה	Psalm	מִזְמוֹר
Food	מַאֲכָל	East	מִזְרָח
To refuse	מָאֵן	Sprinkle bowl	מִזְרָק
To reject	מָאַס	To blot out	מָחָה
Fortified	מִבְצָר	Division	מַחֲלֹקֶת
Tower	מִגְדָּל	Camp	מַחֲנֶה
Shield	מָגֵן	Tomorrow	מָחָר
Plague	מַגֵּפָה	Next day	מָחֳרָת
Pastureland	מִגְרָשׁ	Plans	מַחֲשָׁבָה
Desert	מִדְבָּר	Tribe	מַטֶּה
To measure	מָדַד	Bed	מִטָּה
Measurement	מִדָּה	Rain	מָטָר
Quarrel	מָדוֹן	Who	מִי
Why	מַדּוּעַ	Water	מַיִם
Province	מְדִינָה	Kind	מִין
What	מָה	Wound	מַכָּה
Quickly	מַהֵר	Stand	מְכוֹנָה
To shake	מוֹט	To sell	מָכַר

88

Learn to Read Biblical Hebrew

English	Hebrew	English	Hebrew
To fill	מָלֵא	To be unfaithful	מָעַל
Full	מָלֵא	Unfaithfulness	מַעַל
All in	מָלֵא	Top	מַעַל
Messenger	מַלְאָךְ	Step	מַעֲלָה
Work	מְלָאכָה	Action	מַעֲלָל
Speaking	מִלָּה	So that	מַעַן
Kingdom	מְלוּכָה	Cave	מְעָרָה
Salt	מֶלַח	Work	מַעֲשֶׂה
Battle	מִלְחָמָה	Tenth	מַעֲשֵׂר
To escape	מָלַט	To find	מָצָא
To reign	מָלַךְ	Sacred stone	מַצֵּבָה
King	מֶלֶךְ	Unleavened Brd	מַצָּה
Queen	מַלְכָּה	Command	מִצְוָה
Kingdom	מַלְכוּת	Sanctuary	מִקְדָּשׁ
Kingdom	מַמְלָכָה	Place	מָקוֹם
From	מִן	Livestock	מִקְנֶה
To count	מָנָה	Bitter	מַר
Lampstand	מְנוֹרָה	Appearance	מַרְאֶה
Grain (off.)	מִנְחָה	To rebel	מָרַר
From	מִנִּי	To rebel	מָרָה
To keep	מֶנַע	On high	מָרוֹם
Curtain	מָסָךְ	Chariot	מֶרְכָּבָה
Cast idol	מַסֵּכָה	Deceit	מִרְמָה
Road	מְסִלָּה	Load, oracle	מַשָּׂא
Number	מִסְפָּר	To anoint	מָשַׁח
Stomach	מֵעֶה	Anointed	מָשִׁיחַ
Fortress	מָעוֹז	To pull	מָשַׁךְ
Little	מְעַט	Bed	מִשְׁכָּב
Robe	מְעִיל	Tabernacle	מִשְׁכָּן

Learn to Read Biblical Hebrew

English	Hebrew	English	Hebrew
To rule	מָשַׁל	Noble	נָדִיב
Proverb	מָשָׁל	To make a vow	נָדַר
Duties	מִשְׁמֶרֶת	River	נָהָר
Second	מִשְׁנֶה	To sway	נוּד
Clan	מִשְׁפָּחָה	Pasture	נָוֶה
Justice	מִשְׁפָּט	To give rest	נוּחַ
Weight	מִשְׁקָל	To flee	נוּס
Banquet	מִשְׁתֶּה	To shake	נוּעַ
How long	מָתַי	To wave	נוּף
Please	נָא	Crown	נֵזֶר
Declares	נְאֻם	To lead	נָחָה
To com. adultery	נָאַף	To inherit	נָחַל
To prophecy	נָבָא	Valley	נַחַל
To look	נָבַט	Inheritance	נַחֲלָה
Prophet	נָבִיא	To comfort	נָחַם
Lyre	נֵבֶל	Snake	נָחָשׁ
Dead body	נְבֵלָה	Bronze	נְחֹשֶׁת
South	נֶגֶב	To stretch out	נָטָה
To tell	נָגַד	To plant	נָטַע
in front of	נֶגֶד	To abandon	נָטַשׁ
Ruler	נָגִיד	Pleasing	נִיחֹחַ
To touch	נָגַע	Lamp	נִיר
Mildew	נֶגַע	To strike down	נָכָה
To be defeated	נָגַף	Opposite	נֹכַח
To approach	נָגַשׁ	To recognize	נָכַר
Freewill off.	נְדָבָה	Foriegn	נֵכָר
To flee	נָדַד	Foreigner	נָכְרִי
Monthly period	נִדָּה	To test	נָסָה
To banish	נָדַח	To leave	נָסַע

Learn to Read Biblical Hebrew

English	Hebrew	English	Hebrew
Youth	נְעוּרִים	Booth	סֻכָּה
Young man	נַעַר	To forgive	סָלַח
Young girl	נַעֲרָה	Rocky craig	סֶלַע
To fall	נָפַל	Fine flour	סֹלֶת
Soul	נֶפֶשׁ	To sustain	סָמַךְ
To stand	נָצַב	Threshold	סַף
To supervise	נָצַח	To mourn	סָפַד
Preferred	נֵצַח	To record	סָפַר
To rescue	נָצַל	Scroll	סֵפֶר
To watch	נָצַר	Secretary	סֹפֵר
To be clean	נָקָה	Eunuch	סָרִיס
Innocent	נָקִי	To hide	סָתַר
To avenge	נָקַם	Secret	סֵתֶר
To avenge	נְקָמָה	Think cloud	עָב
To lift up	נָשָׂא	To serve	עָבַד
To overtake	נָשַׂג	Servant	עֶבֶד
Leader	נָשִׂיא	Service	עֲבֹדָה
To kiss	נָשַׁק	For the sake of	עֲבוּר
Eagle	נֶשֶׁר	To cross over	עָבַר
To give	נָתַן	Other side	עֵבֶר
To bring down	נָתַץ	Wrath	עֶבְרָה
To break	נָתַק	Calf	עֵגֶל
To circle round	סָבַב	Ever	עַד
All around	סָבִיב	Until	עַד
To shut	סָגַר	Witness	עֵד
Horse	סוּס	Community	עֵדָה
Reeds	סוּף	Testimony	עֵדוּת
To remove	סוּר	Flock	עֵדֶר
Pot	סִיר	To duplicate	עוּד

91

Learn to Read Biblical Hebrew

English	Hebrew	English	Hebrew
Again	עוֹד	Valley	עֵמֶק
Wicked	עַוְלָה	To answer	עָנָה
Everlasting	עוֹלָם	To humble	עָנָה
Sin	עָוֹן	Humble	עָנָו
To fly	עוּף	Affliction	עֳנִי
Bird	עוֹף	Poor, Humble	עָנִי
To awake	עוּר	Cloud	עָנָן
Skin	עוֹר	Dust	עָפָר
Blind	עִוֵּר	Tree	עֵץ
Goat	עֵז	Counsel	עֵצָה
Strength	עֹז	Strong	עָצוּם
To forsake	עָזַב	Bone	עֶצֶם
To help	עָזַר	To close	עָצַר
Help	עֶזְרָה	Evening	עֶרֶב
Eye	עַיִן	Desert	עֲרָבָה
City	עִיר	Nakedness	עֶרְוָה
On	עַל	To be in order	עָרַךְ
Yoke	עֹל	Value	עֵרֶךְ
To go up	עָלָה	Uncircumcised	עָרֵל
Burnt off.	עֹלָה	Neck	עֹרֶף
Most high	עֶלְיוֹן	Grass	עֵשֶׂב
To close	עָלַם	To do	עָשָׂה
People	עַם	Tenth	עֲשִׂירִי
With	עִם	Smoke	עָשָׁן
To stand	עָמַד	Ten	עֶשֶׂר
With	עִמָּד	Ten	עֶשֶׂר
Near, beside	עֻמָּה	Tenth	עִשָּׂרוֹן
Pillar	עַמּוּד	Twenty	עֶשְׂרִים
Trouble	עָמָל	To oppress	עָשַׁק

Learn to Read Biblical Hebrew

English	Hebrew	English	Hebrew
Wealth	עֹשֶׁר	Punishment	פְּקֻדָּה
Time	עֵת	Bull	פַּר
Now	עַתָּה	To separate	פָּרַד
Goat (m)	עַתּוּד	Fruitful	פָּרָה
Side	פֵּאָה	Cow	פָּרָה
To strike	פָּגַע	To blossom	פָּרַח
To ransom	פָּדָה	Fruit	פְּרִי
Mouth	פֶּה	Curtain	פָּרֹכֶת
Here	פֹּה	To break	פָּרַץ
To scatter	פּוּץ	To break	פָּרַר
To tremble	פָּחַד	To spread	פָּרַשׂ
Fear	פַּחַד	To strip off	פָּשַׁט
Governor	פֶּחָה	To rebel	פָּשַׁע
Concubine	פִּילֶגֶשׁ	Rebellion	פֶּשַׁע
Wonderful	פָּלָא	Sudden	פִּתְאֹם
To deliver	פָּלַט	To deceive	פָּתָה
Remnant	פְּלֵיטָה	To open	פָּתַח
To pray	פָּלַל	Entrance	פֶּתַח
Or	פֶּן	Sheep	צֹאן
To turn	פָּנָה	Army	צָבָא
Corner	פִּנָּה	Side	צַד
Face	פָּנֶה	Righteous	צַדִּיק
Inner	פְּנִימִי	To be righteous	צָדַק
Passover Lamb	פֶּסַח	Righteousness	צֶדֶק
Idol	פֶּסֶל	Righteousness	צְדָקָה
To do	פָּעַל	Neck	צַוָּאר
Deed	פֹּעַל	To command	צִוָּה
Time	פַּעַם	To fast	צוֹם
To punish	פָּקַד	To lay siege	צוּר

English	Hebrew	English	Hebrew
Rock	צוּר	High	קוֹמָה
To prosper	צָלַח	Small	קָטָן
Side	צֵלָע	To burn incense	קָטַר
To grow	צָמַח	Incense	קְטֹרֶת
To cry out	צָעַק	Wall	קִיר
Watchman	צָפָה	To curse	קָלַל
To overlay	צָפָה	Curse	קְלָלָה
North	צָפוֹן	To be jealous	קָנָא
Bird	צִפּוֹר	Jealousy	קִנְאָה
To store up	צָפַן	To buy	קָנָה
Distress	צַר	Rod	קָנֶה
Trouble	צָרָה	End	קֵץ
Disease	צָרַעַת	End	קָצָה
Refine	צָרַף	End	קָצֶה
To be distressed	צָרַר	Harvest	קָצִיר
To assemble	קָבַל	To be angry	קָצַף
To bury	קָבַר	Wrath	קֶצֶף
Grave	קֶבֶר	To harvest	קָצַר
Holy	קָדוֹשׁ	To call	קָרָא
East	קָדִים	To meet	קָרָא
To come, to meet	קֶדֶם	To come near	קָרַב
East, of old	קֶדֶם	Among	קֶרֶב
To consecrate	קָדַשׁ	Offering	קָרְבָּן
Holy	קֹדֶשׁ	To happen	קָרָה
To assemble	קָהַל	Near	קָרוֹב
Assembly	קָהָל	City	קִרְיָה
To bind together	קָוָה	Horn	קֶרֶן
Voice	קוֹל	To tear	קָרַע
To rise up	קוּם	Frame	קֶרֶשׁ

94

English	Hebrew	English	Hebrew
To listen	קָשַׁב	To wash	רָחַץ
Harden	קָשָׁה	To go far	רָחַק
Harsh	קָשֶׁה	To quarrel	רִיב
To conspire	קָשַׁר	Dispute	רִיב
Bow	קֶשֶׁת	Aroma	רֵיחַ
To see	רָאָה	To ride	רָכַב
Head	רֹאשׁ	Chariot	רֶכֶב
First	רִאשׁוֹן	Possession	רְכוּשׁ
First, Beginning	רֵאשִׁית	Pomegranate	רִמּוֹן
Many, Great	רָב	Song of joy	רִנָּה
Many, Great	רֹב	To sing for joy	רָנַן
To increase	רָבָה	Evil	רַע
Fourth	רְבִיעִי	Neighbor	רֵעַ
To lie down	רָבַץ	Famine	רָעָב
To tremble	רָגַז	Shepherd	רָעָה
To spy out	רָגַל	Disaster	רָעָה
Foot	רֶגֶל	To do evil	רָעַע
To pursue	רָדַף	To shake	רָעַשׁ
Wind, spirit	רוּחַ	To heal	רָפָא
To exalt	רוּם	To leave	רָפָה
To shout	רוּעַ	To accept	רָצָה
To run	רוּץ	Will	רָצוֹן
To enlarge	רָחַב	To murder	רָצַח
Street, square	רְחֹב	Only	רַק
Width	רֹחַב	To condemn	רָשַׁע
Far	רָחוֹק	Wicked	רֶשַׁע
To compassion	רָחַם	Wicked	רָשָׁע
Compassion	רַחַם	Grave	שְׁאוֹל
Womb	רֶחֶם	To ask	שָׁאַל

English	Hebrew	English	Hebrew
To remain	שָׁאַר	To laugh	שָׂחַק
Remnant	שְׁאָר	To corrupt	שָׁחַת
Remnant	שְׁאֵרִית	Acacia	שִׁטָּה
To tk captive	שָׁבָה	Accuser, Satan	שָׂטָן
Oath	שְׁבוּעָה	To sweep away	שָׁטַף
Fortune	שְׁבוּת	Official	שֹׁטֵר
Tribe	שֵׁבֶט	To sing	שִׁיר
Captivity	שְׁבִי	Song	שִׁיר
Seventh	שְׁבִיעִי	To set	שִׁית
To swear	שָׁבַע	To lie down	שָׁכַב
To satisfy	שָׂבַע	To forget	שָׁכַה
Seven	שֶׁבַע	To be wise	שָׂכַל
To break	שָׁבַר	To get up early	שָׁכַם
Destruction	שֶׁבֶר	To dwell	שָׁכַן
To stop, end	שָׁבַת	Wages, Reward	שָׂכָר
Sabbath	שַׁבָּת	Fullness, Peace	שָׁלוֹם
Destruction	שֹׁד	Three	שָׁלוֹשׁ
To destroy	שָׁדַד	To send	שָׁלַח
Field	שָׂדֶה	Table	שֻׁלְחָן
Almighty	שַׁדַּי	Third	שְׁלִישִׁי
Sheep	שֶׂה	To throw	שָׁלַךְ
Vain	שָׁרִי	Plunder	שָׁלָל
To return	שׁוּב	To make full	שָׁלַם
To put, set	שִׂים	Peace off.	שֶׁלֶם
Gatekeeper	שׁוֹעֵר	To draw	שָׁלַף
Ram's horn	שׁוֹפָר	Three days	שִׁלְשׁוֹם
Ox	שׁוֹר	There	שָׁם
To rejoice	שׂוּשׂ	Name	שֵׁם
To slaughter	שָׁחַט	Left	שְׂמֹאל

Learn to Read Biblical Hebrew

English	Hebrew	English	Hebrew
To destroy	שָׁמַד	To bring low	שָׁפֵל
Desolate	שַׁמָּה	To give drink	שָׁקָה
News	שְׁמוּעָה	Detestable	שִׁקּוּץ
To rejoice	שָׂמַח	To be quiet	שָׁקַט
Joy	שִׂמְחָה	Shekel	שֶׁקֶל
Heaven	שָׁמַיִם	Untruth	שֶׁקֶר
Eighth	שְׁמִינִי	Official	שַׂר
Clothes	שִׂמְלָה	Survivor	שָׂרִיד
To be desolate	שָׁמֵם	To burn	שָׂרַף
Desolate	שְׁמָמָה	Root	שֹׁרֶשׁ
Oil	שֶׁמֶן	To minister	שָׁרַת
Eight	שְׁמֹנֶה	Linen	שֵׁשׁ
To hear	שָׁמַע	Six	שֵׁשׁ
To keep	שָׁמַר	Sixth	שִׁשִּׁי
Sun	שֶׁמֶשׁ	To drink	שָׁתָה
Teeth	שֵׁן	Fig	תְּאֵנָה
To hate	שָׂנֵא	Ark	תֵּבָה
Year	שָׁנָה	Harvest	תְּבוּאָה
Scarlet	שָׁנִי	Understanding	תְּבוּנָה
Second	שֵׁנִי	World	תֵּבֵל
Two	שְׁנַיִם	Deep	תְּהוֹם
Goat	שָׂעִיר	Praise	תְּהִלָּה
Gate	שַׁעַר	Thanksgiving	תּוֹדָה
Hair	שֵׂעָר	Center	תָּוֶךְ
Barley	שְׂעֹרָה	Geneology	תֹּלְדוֹת
Lip, Edge	שָׂפָה	Worm	תּוֹלֵעָה
Maidservant	שִׁפְחָה	Detestable	תּוֹעֵבָה
To deliver	שָׁפַט	Out	תֵּצֵאוֹת
To pour out	שָׁפַךְ	Torah	תּוֹרָה

English	Hebrew
To plea	תְּחִנָּה
Under	תַּחַת
New wine	תִּירוֹשׁ
Blue	תְּכֵלֶת
To hang	תָּלָה
Blameless	תֹּם
Regular	תָּמִיד
Without defect	תָּמִים
To be perfect	תָּמַם
Wave off.	תְּנוּפָה
To stray	תָּעָה
Glorious	תִּפְאֶרֶת
Prayer	תְּפִלָּה
To seize	תָּפַשׂ
Hope	תִּקְוָה
To blow	תָּקַע
Offering	תְּרוּמָה
Shout, Trumpet	תְּרוּעָה
Deliverance	תְּשׁוּעָה
Nine	תֵּשַׁע

Part 6
Parent / Child Roots

The most ancient Hebrew words are all derived from a tw-letter parent root such as בל (flow). A child root is formed by placing a vowel (י, ו, ה, א) in front, between or at the end of the two letters of the parent root. The following child roots are derived from the parent בל meaning, "flow."

אבל (wilt; a flowing away of life)
הבל (empty; a flowing away of contents)
בהל (panic; a flowing of the insides)
בלה (aged; a flowing away of youth)
בול (flood; a heavy flowing of water)
יבל (stream; a flowing of water).

As you will notice, all the child roots are related in meaning to each other and the parent root.

Since approximately 80% of the Hebrew words in the Bible are a parent or child root or a word derived from these roots, it is relatively easy to find the meaning of a word based on the root of the word. For example the child root ראש has the meaning of "head" or "top." The words ראשון, ראשית and ראשה are derived from this child root and all have a meaning of "the head or top of something." At times the meaning of a word derived from the root appear to be very different from the root. This is due to our modern understanding of words, which are often times very different from the ancient Hebrews understanding of words. When the word does not appear to be related, a more concise dictionary should be consulted.

The following list will only include those roots whose words derived from it are found in the Hebrew Bible. For example, the two words מבון and תבון are found in the Hebrew Bible and are derived from the child root בון. The following list will include the entry בון but not מבון and תבון.

Occasionally a letter of a word will change to another letter of a similar sound but will retain a meaning resembling the original root. For example the root כור (kor; meaning dig) has evolved into the following forms.

קור (qor)   גור (gor)   חור (chor)   בור (bor)   עור (ghor)

Each of these words is similar in sound and each have the meaning of "dig" and will be included under the child root of כור. In this case, the entry קור will have the word כור to the right, indicating that you will find this word there.

אב	
Father	אב
Bear fruit	אבב
Wineskin, medium	אוב
Desire	יאב
Hostile, enemy	איב
אד	
Fog, mist	אד
Befall	אדד
Fire poker	אוד
Calamity	איד
אה	
Desire	אה
Desire	או
Desire	אי
Desire	אוה
Desire	יאה
Desire	איה
אז	
Time, place	אז
אח	
Brother, hearth	אח
אט	
Gentle	אט
אך	
כן	אך
אל	
God, chief	אל
Strong	אלל
Oath	אלה
Strong	אול

Begin	יאל
אם	
Mother, if	אם
Cubit, community	אמם
Bondwoman	אמה
אן	
Idol, nothing	אן
Idol, nothing	אנן
Idol, nothing	אין
אף	
Nose, anger	אף
Aroma, baking	אפה
אץ	
Press	אוץ
אר	
Light	אור
אש	
Fire	אש
Foundation, cake	אשש
Foundation	אשה
Despair	יאש
את	
Mark, with, plow	את
Mark	אתא
Arrive, you	אתה
Mark	אות
בב	
Pupil of the eye	בבה
Cry out	יבב
בד	
Alone, branch	בד

Alone, branch	בדד	Flow	יבל
Wander	אבד	**בם**	
Lie	בדא	High	בהם
בה		High	במה
Void	בהה	Brother-in-law	יבם
Need	אבה	**בן**	
Come	בוא	Son	בן
בז		Stone	אבן
Plunder	בז	Thumb	בהן
Plunder	בזז	Structure, children	בנה
Plunder	בזא	intelligence	בון
Plunder	בזה	Seperate	בין
Plunder	בוז	**בס**	
בח		Trample	בוס
Remain	אבח	**בע**	
בט		Gush, request	בעה
Marble	בהט	**בץ**	
Idle talk	בטה	White clay	בץ
בך		Swamp	בצץ
Roll, swell	אבך	White, linen, egg	בוץ
Weep	בכא	**בק**	
Weep	בכה	Pour out, destroy	בקק
Wander	בוך	Powder, dust	אבק
בל		Rash	בהק
Nothing	בל	Empty	בוק
Mixture	בלל	**בר**	
Lamend	אבל	Clean, soap, grain	בר
Vain, empty	הבל	Clean, pure	ברר
Panic, anticipation	בהל	Strong wing	אבר
Fail, aged	בלה	באר	כר
Flood	בול	Fat	ברא

Learn to Read Biblical Hebrew

White	בהר	Back, body	גוה	
Food, soap	ברה	Grieve	יגה	
כר	בור	Valley	גיה	

בש	
Shame, dried up	בוש
Shame	ביש

בת	
Defined	בתת
Desolate	בתה
Household	בית

גב	
Bent back, dig	גב
Cistern	גבא
High	גבה
Locust, cut, dig	גוב
Dig	יגב

גג	
Roof	גג

גד	
Attack, troop	גד
Attack, furrow	גדד
Troop, band	אגד
Riverbank	גדה
Attack, troop	גוד
Tendon	גיד

גה	
Pride	גא
Back	גו
Valley	גי
Pride	גאה
Heal	גהה

Back, body	גוה
Grieve	יגה
Valley	גיה
Back, body	גף
Arch, body	גוף

גז	
Fleece, mow	גז
Sheer	גזז
Fleece	גזה
Sweep	גוז

גל	
Round, role, stone	גל
Round, role, log	גלל
Collect	אגל
Redeem	גאל
Naked, exile	גלה
Rejoice, fear	גול
2nd time around	עלל

גם	
Also	גם
Marsh	אגם
Drink, reed	גמא
Gather	גמה

גן	
Garden	גן
Protect	גנן
Bowl	אגן

גע	
Gasp	יגע
Bellow	געה

Last breath	גוע

גף	
גה	גף
גה	גוף
Non-native, chalk	גר
Throat, drag	גרר
Gather, collect	אגר
Prostrate	גהר
Anger	גרה
Fear, guest	גור
Fear	יגר
Plaster	גיר

גש	
Grope	גשש
Cloud	גיש

גת	
Winepress	גת
Slow	דב
Slow	דבב
Flow	דאב
Sluggish	דבא
Mope	דוב

דג	
Fish	דג
anxious	דאג
Increase	דגה
Fishing	דוג

דד	
Breasts	דד
Gentle walk	דדה
Pot, basket, uncle	דיד

דה	
Enough	די
Dart	דאה
Sick	דוה
Rapid flight	דיה

דח	
Thrust	דחח
Push down	דחה
Push away	דוח

דך	
Crush	דך
Trample	דכא
Collaps	דכה
Crush	דוך

דל	
Dangle	דל
Week, poor	דלל
Draw water	דלה

דם	
Blood	דם
Silent	דמם
Red, man	אדם
Silent	דהם
Likeness, silent	דמה

דן	
Ruler, lord	אדן
Quarrel	דון
Rule	דין

דע	
Know	דע
Inteligence	דוע

Know	ידע		Shout	הדד
דף			Stretch out hand	הדה
Push	דפה		Splendor	הוד
דץ			**הה**	
Leap	דוץ		Behold, look	הה
דק			Behold, look	הא
Thin, canopy	דק		Behold, look	הו
Crumble	דקק		Behold, look	הי
Crumble	דיק		He, she	הוא
דר			Grief, desire	הוה
Circle, round	דר		Exist	היה
Swallow, free	דרר		**הז**	
Wide	אדר		Dream	הזה
Wide	דאר		**הל**	
Turn, honor	הדר		Shine	הלל
Gallop	דהר		Tent	אהל
circle, generation	דור		Far away	הלא
דש			**הם**	
Sprout	דשא		Abundant, rich	הם
Tread	דוש		Commotion	המם
דת			Noise	המה
Law	דת		Uproar	הום
הב			**הן**	
Privelidge	הב		Behold, here, if	הן
Love, affection	אהב		Heavy, rich	הון
Give	יהב		Hin (a measure)	הין
הג			**הס**	
Meditate	הגג		Still	הס
Murmer, remove	הגה		Silent, still	הסה
הד			**הר**	
Shout	הד		Mount, hill	הר

High, arrogant	הרר		**זל**	
Pregnant	הרה	Shake		זלל
High	יהר	Depart		אזל
הת		Except		זול
Break in, assail	התת	Shake, settle		צלל
וו		**זם**		
hood, peg, nail	וו	Plan		זמם
זב		**זן**		
Hyssop	אזב	Kinds		זן
Gold, yellow	זהב	Heavy, stout		יזן
Puss	זוב	Broad, ear		אזן
Gold	צהב	Whoredom		זנה
זג		Fat		זון
Grapeskin	זג	**זע**		
זד		Tremble		זוע
Waves, soup	זד	Sweat		יזע
Waves, soup	זוד	**זף**		
זה		Flow		זוף
This	זה	Sheet over		צפה
Shine, beauty	זהה	Overflow		צוף
סה	זוה	**זק**		
זז		Fuse, refine		זק
Move, rich	זוז	Chains		זקק
זח		**זר**		
Remove	זחח	Stranger		זר
זך		Sneeze		זרר
Clear	זך	צר		זרר
Clear	זכך	צר		אזר
Pure	זכה	Loath, turn away		זאר
		Warn		זהר

Scatter, winnow	זרה		**חז**	
Loath, turn away	זור	Gaze	חזז	
צר	זור	Possess	אחז	
זת		Gaze	חזה	
Olive	זית	Enclose	חוז	
חב		**חח**		
Bosom	חב	Thistle, hook	חח	
Bosom	חבב	Hook	חוח	
Refuge, secret	חבא	**חט**		
Hide	חבה	Miss, sin	חטא	
Debt	חוב	Cord	חוט	
חג		**חך**		
Festival	חג	Roof of the mouth	חך	
Festival	חגג	Wait	חכה	
Revolve	חגא	**חל**		
Refuge	חגה	Common	חל	
Circle	חוג	Common, pierce	חלל	
חד		Sick, rust	חלא	
Unite	חד	Sick, pierce	חלה	
Unite	חדד	Turn	חול	
One, unite	אחד	חר	יחל	
Glad	חדה	**חם**		
Riddle	חוד	Hot	חם	
Unite	יחד	Hot	חמם	
חה		Curdled	חמא	
Life	חה	Wall	חמה	
Life	חי	Burned, black	חום	
Life	חוה	Passion, anger	יחם	
Life	חיה	**חן**		
Life	חיי	Camp, grace	חן	

Camp, grace	חָנַן	Wait	יָחַר
Pole, spear	חֲנָה	Patient	יָחַל
Camp, grace	חוּן	**חשׁ**	
חס		Quiet	חָשָׁה
Trust, refuge	חָסָה	Hurry	חוּשׁ
Compassion	חוּס	Lineage	יָחַשׂ
חף		Hurry	עוּשׁ
Clean, pure	חַף	**חת**	
Secret	חָפָא	Break, crumble	חַת
Clean, pure	חָפַף	Break, crumble	חָתַת
Cover, protect	חָפָה	Sieze	חָתָה
Haven	חוּף	**טב**	
חץ		Good	טָב
Arrow	חֵץ	Good	יָטַב
Divide, arrow	חָצַץ	Good	טוֹב
Half	חָצָה	**טד**	
Outside	חוּץ	Thorn	אָטָד
Wall	חִיץ	**טה**	
חק		Spun	טָוָה
Appointment	חֹק	Sweep	טוּא
Appoint, inscribe	חָקַק	**טח**	
Inscribe	חָקָה	Lay out, kidney	טָחָה
Bosom	חוֹק	Overlay	טוּח
חר		**טט**	
Glow hot, noble	חָר	Mud	טִט
Heated by the sun	חָרַר	**טל**	
Remain, after	אָחַר	Dew	טַל
Dung, privy	חָרָא	Covering	טָלַל
Anger	חָרָה	Cover	טָלָא
White	חוּר	Spotting	טָלָה
כוּר	חוֹר	Strew	טוּל

108

	טם
Unclean	טם
Unclean	טמא
Unclean	טמה

	טן
Basket	טנא

	טע
Wander	טעה

	טף
Children	טף
Trip	טפף
Surround	טוף

	טר
Closed	אטר
Pure	טהר
Wall	טור

	טש
Pounce	טוש

	יג
Grieve	יגה

	יד
Hand	יד
Handle	ידד
Hand out	ידה

	ים
Sea	ים
Terror	אים
Day	יום

	ין
Mud	יון
Wine	יין

	יע
Shovel	יע
Brush	יעה

	יף
Beauty	יפה

	יר
River	יאר
Fear	ירא
Point, rain, teach	ירה

	יש
Exist	יש
Aged	ישש
Exist	ישה

	כב
Pain	כאב
Extinguish	כבה

	כד
Jar	כד
Strike	כדד
Strike	כיד

	כה
Brand	כי
Sespond	כאה
Weak	כהה
Burn	כוה

	כח
Strength	כח
Chastise	יכח

	כל
Complete	כל
Complete	כלל

Eat	אכל	קר	כרה
Keep	כלא	Dig	כור
Complete	כלה	Hole	באר
Sustain	כול	Dig	בור
Able, Could	יכל	Dig	חור
כם		Dig	עור
Desire, long for	כמה	Trench	קור
כן		**כש**	
Stand upright	כן	כס	כשה
Plant	כנן	Terror	כוש
Priest	כהן	**כת**	
Eulogy	כנה	Crush	כתת
Stand	כון	**לב**	
Sure	אך	Heart	לב
כס		Heart	לבב
Estimate	כסס	Thirst	לאב
Covering	כסא	Lion	לבא
Cover	כסה	Glisten	להב
Cup, pocket	כוס	Lion	לבה
Fat	כשה	**לג**	
Cup	קוס	Log (measure)	לג
כף		Study	להג
Palm	כף	**לד**	
Bend	כפף	Offspring, child	ילד
Bow	אכף	Offspring, child	ולד
Tame	כפה	**לה**	
כר		If, no, not	לא
Leap,cor(measure)	כר	If	לו
Leap	כרר	Weary, faint	לאה
Farm	אכר	Weary, faint	להה
Dig	כרה	Nothing, foolish	אל

Nothing, foolish	אלל		לם
Nothing, foolish	אול	Silent, tied up	אלם
Nothing, foolish	יאל	Community	לאם

לה	
Join, lend	לוה
If	לוא

לן	
Encamp	לון

לז	
Turn aside	לזה
Turn aside	לוז

לע	
Throat	לע
Swallow	לוע
Blurt	ילע

לח	
Moist, fresh	לח
Cheek	לחה
Corrupt	אלח
Clay tablet	לוח
Lick	לק

לץ	
Mock, interpret	ליץ
Urge	אלץ
Mock, interpret	לוץ

לק	
לח	לק

לט	
Veil	לט
Veil, cover	לאט
Lizard	לטא
Flames	להט
Secret, cover	לוט

לש	
Knead	לוש

מג	
Magi	מג
Melt	מוג

לך	
Messenger	לאך
Walk	הלך
Walk	ילך

מד	
Carpet, measure	מד
Carpet, measure	מדד
Extend	מדה
Stretch out	מוד

לל	
Howl	אלל
Loop	ללא
Stairway	לול
Howl	ילל
Night	ליל

מה	
What	מה
What	מו
Who	מי
Hundred	מאה

Learn to Read Biblical Hebrew

Question	מהה	Spurn	מאס

מח		מסה Disolve, faint	
Marrow, rich	מח		
Marrow	מחח		

		מע	
Strike	מחא	Bowels, soft	מע
Strike	מחה	Bowels, soft	מעה

מט		מץ	
Shake, yoke	מוט	Chaff, oppression	מץ
Branch	מטה	Suck, matsa	מצץ

מך		Strong	אמץ
Thin, poor	מך	Find	מצא
Thin, poor	מכך	Suck	מצה

		Chaff, oppression	מוץ

מל		מק	
Reduce, discourse	מלל	Dissipate	מק
Sick	אמל	Dissipate	מקק
Fill	מלא	Mock	מוק
Reduce	מהל		
uncircumcised	מול		

		מר	
		Bitter, rebel	מר

מם		Bitter, rebel	מרר
Blemish	מאם	Say	אמר

מן		Bitter, rebel	מאר
Kind, from	מן	Hurry, exchange	מהר
Kind, from	מנן	Bitter, rebel	מרה
Strong	אמן	Exchange	מור
Refuse	מאן	Exchange	ימר
Assign, count	מנה		

Likeness	מון	משׁ	
Right hand	ימן	Grope	משׁשׁ

מס		Drawn out	משׁה
Disolve, faint	מס	Drawn out	מושׁ
Disolve, faint	מסס	Grope	ימשׁ

112

Learn to Read Biblical Hebrew

	מת
Death	מת
Death	מות
Death	מתה

	נב
Bore	נבב
Prophecy	נבא
High	נבה
Produce	נונ

	נג
Drive	נהג
Bright	נגה

	נד
Flee, wander	נד
Flee, wander	נדד
Toss about	נדה
Flee, wander	נוד

	נה
Please	נא
Lament	ני
sit, dwell	נאה
Lament	נהה
sit, dwell	נוה
Disposses	ינה
Forbid	נוא
Raw	ניא

	נז
Sprinkle	נזה

	נח
Sigh	אנח
Lead	נחה

Rest	נוח

	נט
Spread out	נטה
Shake	נוט

	נך
Beat	נכא
Beat	נכה

	נל
Complete	נלה
Rubble	נול

	נם
Sleep	נום

	נן
Sprout, continue	נון

	נס
Flag	נס
Beacon, glee	נסס
	נסס
Test	נסה
Flee	נוס
Lift up	נשא

	נע
Shake	נוע

	נף
Wave	נוף

	נץ
Shine	נצץ
Dispise	נאץ
Fly	נצא
Quarrel	נצה
Fly away	נוץ

113

Learn to Read Biblical Hebrew

נק	
Cry out	אנק
Cry out	נהק
Innocent	נקה
Suckle	נוק
Suckle	ינק

נר	
Lamp	נר
River	נהר
Lamp, yoke	נור

נש	
Lend	נשא
Lend	נשה
Sick	נוש
Sick	נסס

סב	
Turn	סבב
Drunk	סבא
Old	שיב

סד	
Foundation	סד
Assembly	סוד
Foundation	יסד
Level	שדד
Witness	שהד
Field	שדה
Plaster	שיד

סה	
seah (measure)	סאה
Veil	סוה
Sheep	שה

Forget	שי
Forget	שהה
Rise	שוא
Elevate	שיא
Conceal, hide	זוה

סח	
Sweep away	שחה
Meditate	שה
Swim, float	שחה
Meditate	שוח
Ponder, plant	שיח

סט	
Turn aside	סט
	שט
Depart	סוט
Turn aside	שט
Deviate	שטה
Turn aside	שוט

סך	
Booth	סך
Cover	סכך
Anoint	סוך
Thorn, hedge	שך
Cover, thorn	שכך
View	שכה
Cover	שוך

סל	
Raise, basket	סל
Raise	סלל
Weigh	סלא
Raise	סלה

Quail	שׁלו	**סק**	
סם		Sack	שׂק
Smell	סם	Sack	שׂקק
Smell	סמם	**סר**	
Storehouse	אסם	Sad, anger	סר
Poison	שׁמם	Sad, anger	סרר
Garlic	שׁום	Bind, yoke	אסר
סן		Round	סהר
Shoe	סאן	Instruct	יסר
Thistle	סנא	pot, fishhook	סיר
Thorn	צן	Commander	שׂר
Sharp, protect	צנן	Rule	שׂרר
Flock	צאן	Bind	אשׂר
Flock	צון	Yeast	שׂאר
Thistle	סנה	Rule	שׂור
Hate	שׂנא	**סת**	
סס		Winter	סתה
Cheerful, moth	סס	Entice	סות
Horse, swallow	סוס	**עב**	
Cheerful	שׂוש	Dark covering	עב
סע		Thick, dense	עבה
Rush	סעה	Dark covering	עוב
סף		**עג**	
Lip, edge	סף	Baked bread	עוג
Door	ספף	**עד**	
Take, gather	אסף	Appointed time	עדד
Feed	ספא	Pass, ornament	עדה
Scrape	ספה	Testify, witness	עוד
Take, gather	יסף	Appointed	יעד
Lip	שׂפה		

Learn to Read Biblical Hebrew

	עה		Watch, depress	עָנָה
Evil	עָו		Abode	עוֹן
Ruins	עִי		Watch	יַעַן
Sweep away	יָעָה		Eye	עַיִן

	עז			עס
Goat	עֵז		Tread	עָסַס
Strong	עָזַז		Do	עָשָׂה
Bold	עַזָּה			עף
Stronghold	עוֹז		Branch	עַפָה
Strong	יָעֹז		Fly	עוּף

	עט		Exhausted	יָעַף
Stylus, pen	עֵט		Exhausted	עָיֵף
Wrap	עָטָה			עץ
Dig in	עוּט		Tree	עֵץ
Wrap	יָעַט		Spine	עֻצָה
Bird of prey	עַיִט		Counsel	עוּץ
עִיץ	יַעַט		Counsel	יָעַץ

	על		Counsel	יַעַט
Yoke, top, high	עֹל			עק
Work	עָלַל		Parepet	עֲקָה
גַּל	עָלַל		Oppress	עוּק
Ascend	עָלָה			ער
Give milk	עוּל		Enemy, bare	עַר
Ascend	יַעַל		Naked	עָרַר

	עם		Naked	עָרָה
Flock, with	עַם		Watch, wake, bare	עוּר
Hidden	עָמַם		כוּר	עוּר
Neighbor	עָמָה		Forest	יַעַר
Violence	עִים			עש

	ען		Waste away	עָשַׁשׁ
Cover, cloud	עָנָן		עס	עָשָׂה

116

עוש	חש

עת	
Help	עות

פג	
Unripe, unfit	פג
Unripe, unfit	פגג
Unripe, unfit	פוג

פד	
Girdle	אפד
Redeem	פדה
Disappear	פוד

פה	
Mouth, edge, word	פה
Beard, blow	פאה
Beard, blow	פיה

פז	
Refine	פז
Refine, leap	פזז

פח	
Spread	פח
Net	פחח
Governor	פחה
Blow, dust	פוח
Breathe	יפח

פך	
Flask	פך
Overturn	הפך
Pour	פכה
Eye paint	פוך

פל	
Intercede	פלל

Darkness	אפל
Wonder	פלא
Wonder	פלה
Bean	פול

פם	
Fat	פים

פן	
Face, turn	פן
Face, turn	פנן
Wheel	אפן
Face	פנה
Turn	פון

פס	
Ankle, wrist, end	פס
Ankle, wrist, end	פסס
Ankle, wrist	אפס

פע	
Viper	אפע
Quiet scream	פעה

פץ	
Disperse, scatter	פצץ
Open	פצה
Scatter	פוץ

פק	
Restrain	אפק
Waver, unsteady	פוק

פר	
Bull	פר
Break	פרר
Abundance, dust	אפר
Adorn, honor	פאר

כר	פאר	Glare	צחח
Wild donkey	פרא	Dig	צחה
Fruit	פרה	Cry out	צוח
Winepress	פור	Desert	ציח

פש		**צל**	
Leopresy	פשה	Shade	צל
Spread	פוש	Shade	צלל

פת		זל	צלל
Pudenda, socket	פת	Near	אצל
Entice	פתה	Neigh	צהל

צב		Roast	צלה
Wall	צב	Deep	צול

		צם	
Army	צבא	Cover the mouth	צמם
זב	צהב	Thirst	צמא
Swell	צבה	Fast	צום
Stand erect	יצב		

צג		**צן**	
Set	יצג	סן	צן

צד		סן	צנן
Side	צד	סן	צאן
Lay down	צדה	סן	צון
Hunt	צוד		

צה		**צע**	
Issue	צא	Wander	צעה
Command	צו	Sheet, floor	יצע

Ship	צי	**צף**	
Command	צוה	Whisper	צפף
Desert, nomad	ציה	Watch	צפה
Issue	צוא	זף	צפה

צח		זף	צוף
Desert	צח	**צץ**	

		Blossom	צוץ

	צק
Funnel	צוק
Pour	יצק

	צר
Wraped, pressed	צר
Wraped, pressed	צרר
Store up	אצר
Pain	צאר
Olive oil	צהר
Pressed, rock	צור
Pressed	יצר
Journey	ציר
Bind	זרר
Bind	אזר
Press	זור
Lie in wait	שרר

	צת
Kindle	צות
Kindle	יצת

	קב
Jar, tent, belly	קב
Jar, tent, belly	קבב

	קד
Bow the head	קדד
Burn	יקד

	קה
Cord	קו
Gourd	קי
Dull	קהה
Cord, collect	קוה
Obey	יקה

Vomit	קיה
Vomit	קוא

	קט
Little	קט
Cut off	קטט
Cut off	קוט

	קל
Light, quick	קל
Light, quick	קלל
Assemble	קהל
Roast	קלה
Voice, sound	קול

	קם
Raise	קום

	קן
Nest	קן
Nest	קנן
Jealous	קנא
Acquire	קנה
lament	קין

	קס
כס	קסס
קץ	קוס

	קע
Brand	קוע
Hang, shrivel	יקע

	קף
Condense	קפא
Go around	קוף

	קץ
Cut, end	קץ

Cut, end	קצה		**רד**	
Cut, end, loathe	קוץ	Tread	רדד	
Cut	קסס	Flee	ארד	
קר		Tread	דרה	
Cool, quiet	קר	Wander	רוד	
Meet, call	קרא	Descend	ירד	
Meet	קרה	**רה**		
Precious	יקר	Rain	רי	
Purchase	כרה	Lion, box	ארה	
כר	קור	See	ראה	
קש		Fear, awe	רהה	
Straw, bend	קש	Rain	רוה	
Gather	קשש	Fear, awe	ירה	
Melon	קשא	Fear, awe	ירא	
Hard	קשה	**רז**		
Bend	קוש	Ceder	ארז	
Snare	יקש	Thin	רזה	
רב		**רח**		
Abundant	רב	Traveler	ארח	
Abundant	רבב	Handmill	רחה	
Ambush	ארב	Wind, spirit	רוח	
Bold	רהב	Moon	ירח	
Abundant	רבה	**רט**		
Defend, quarrel	רוב	Trough	רהט	
רג		Cast down	ירט	
Weave	ארג	**רך**		
Kill	הרג	Loins	רך	
Bad, loud	רע	Loins	רכך	
Bad, break	רעע	Long	ארך	
Loud	רוע	**רם**		
Break up	ירע	Lift up, worm	רמם	

Lift up	אָרַם	Accept	רצה
Lift up	רֹאם	Run	רוץ
Throw, betray	רמה		**רק**
Lift up	רום	Thin, spit	רק
Lift up	ירם	Thin, spit	רקק
	רן	Empty	רוק
Shout	רן	Spit, green	ירק
Shout	רנן		**רר**
Nimble	ארן	Spit	רר
Rattle	רנה	Curse	ארר
	רס	Spit, egg white	רור
Dew, pieces	רסס		**רש**
Betroth	ארס	Divide	רשש
Break, pull down	הרס	Request	ארש
Betroth	ארש	רס	ארש
	רע	Head	ראש
Companion	רע	Permission	רשא
רג	רע	Permission	רשה
רג	רעע	Needy	רוש
Shepherd	רעה	Possession	ירש
רג	רוע		**שב**
רג	ירע	Split	שבב
	רף	שק	שאב
Heal	רפא	Captive	שבה
Feeble	רפה	Turn back	שוב
Pulverize	רוף	Sit, dwell	ישב
	רץ	סב	שיב
Pieces	רץ		**שג**
Broken pieces	רצץ	Mistake	שגג
Land	ארץ	Groan	שאג
Run	רצא	Mistake	שגא

121

Mistake	שגה	**שט**	
Mistake	שוג	שט	סט
שד		Flog	שטט
Breast, goat	שד	Despise	שאט
Power	שדד	Accasia tree	שטה
שדד	סד	שטה	סט
Ravine	אשד	lash, whip	שוט
שהד	סד	שוט	סט
שדה	סד	Stretch out	ישט
Power	שוד	**שך**	
שיד	סד	שך	סך
שה		Bow down, lower	שכך
שה	סה	שכך	סך
Gift	שי	Wander	שכה
שי	סה	שכה	סך
Storm	שאה	שוך	סך
Storm	שוה	**של**	
False	שוא	Draw out	של
שיא	סה	Plunder	שלל
שוא	סה	Tamerisk tree	אשל
שח		Ask	שאל
Pit, bow	שח	Draw out	שלה
שח	סח	Shirt	שול
Pit, bow, submit	שחח	שלו	סל
Pit, bow	שחה	**שם**	
שחה	סח	Name	שם
Pit, bow	שוח	Desolate	שמם
שוח	סח	שמם	סם
Empty	ישח	Guilt	אשם
שיח	סח	High	שמא

Onyx	שהם	**שק**	
High	שמה	Leg	שק
Garlic	שום	סק	שק
ס̄ם	שום	Greed, eager	שקק
Desolate	ישם	סק	שקק
שׁן		Drink	שקה
Teeth	שן	Leg, trough, street	שוק
Sharp	שנן	**שר**	
סן	שנא	Cord, rope, sinew	שר
Rest, quiet	שאן	סר	שר
Repeat, year	שנה	Twist together	שרר
Urine	שון	צר	שרר
Sleep	ישן	סר	שרר
שׂם		Happy	אשר
Plunder	שסס	סר	אשר
Plunder	שאס	Relative	שאר
Plunder	שסה	סר	שאר
Plunder	שוס	Untie	שרה
שׂע		Over, wall	שור
Delight, blind	שעע	סר	שור
Watch	שעה	Straight	ישר
Cry out, deliver	שוע	Song	שיר
Free, safe	ישע	**שׁש**	
שׁף		White, six	שש
Serpent	שפף	Lead, drag	ששא
Quiver	אשף	White	שוש
Draw in wind	שאף	סס	שוש
Stand out	שפה	Old man	ישש
סף	שפה	**שׁת**	
Strike	שוף	Buttock, foundation	שת
Draw in	שאב	Banquet	שתה

Set	שִׁית

תב	
Box	תֵבָה

תד	
Peg, stake	יָתֵד

תה	
Room	תָא
Mark, sign	תָו
mark, sign	תָאָה
Empty	תֹהַה
Mark, sign	תָוָה
Empty	תֹהוּ

תח	
Sink down, bow	תּוּחַ

תך	
Oppress, bend	תֹךְ
Oppress, bend	תָכַךְ
Bow down, sit	תָכָה
Middle	תָוֶךְ

תל	
Mound	תֵל
Mound	תָלַל
Hang, suspend	תָלָא
Hang, suspend	תָלָה

תם	
Whole, full	תָם
Whole, full	תָמַם
Twins	תָאַם
Amaze	תָמַה

תן	
Patient, monster	תַן
Patient, monster	תָנַן
Gift, wage, donkey	אֶתַן
Gift, wage	תָנָה
Permanent, river	יָתַן

תף	
Drum	תֹף
Beat	תָפַף
Spit	תּוּף

תר	
Outline	תָאַר
Travel	תּוּר
Remain, much	יָתַר

תש	
He-goat	תַיִשׁ

Part 7
Adopted Roots

Adopted roots are three consonant roots that evolved out of the parent or child root. This list includes all the adopted roots where all the words derived from it are used more than 25 times inclusively, in the Hebrew Bible.

Just as in the parent and child root list, this list only contains the root and not the words derived from it, though the words are closely related in meaning to the adopted root.

While 80% of the words in the Bible are words derived from the parent or child roots, another 15% are derived from these adopted roots providing a fairly comprehensive root dictionary.

Learn to Read Biblical Hebrew

English	Root	English	Root
thousand, chief, join	אלף	bent, vine	גפן
covering, clothing	בגד	angry, stone, lots	גרל
seperate	בדל	level, threshing floor	גרן
choose, select	בחר	take away, detract	גרע
cling, trust, secure	בטח	cast out	גרש
firstborn, firstfruit	בכר	rain	גשם
wallow, destroy	סבלע	adhere	דבק
distant, behind	בעד	speak, order	דבר
lord, husband	בעל	honey	דבש
burn, destroy	בער	weep	דמע
break, cut, plunder	בצע	tread, way, walk	דרך
cut off the vine	בצר	fat	דשן
break through/open	בקע	slaughter, sacrifice	זבח
plow, cattle	בקר	remember, male	זכר
seek, request	בקש	cut, divide, sing	זמר
iron	ברזל	angry, insolent	זעם
pass, flee	ברח	call out, assemble	זעק
knee, bless	ברך	beard, chin, old	זקן
boil, ripen	בשל	rise	זרח
sweet, pleasent	בשם	scatter, sow, seed	זרע
flesh, good news	בשר	scatter, dish	זרק
boundary	גבל	writh, twist, bind	חבל
high, hill	גבע	bind, join	חבר
strong, warrior	גבר	bind, gird	חבש
great	גדל	bind, gird	חגר
wall, fence	גדר	cease, omit	חדל
cut off/down, divide	גזד	enclise, chamber	חדר
ripe, wean, camel	גמל	new	חדש
steal	גנב	strong	חזק
rebuke, reproof	גער	fat	חלב

126

Learn to Read Biblical Hebrew

English	Root	English	Root
fat, dream	חלם	taste, decree	טעם
pass by	חלף	not yet	טרם
smooth	חלק	tear in pieces, feed	טרף
desire	חמד	heavy, honor, liver	כבד
compassion	חמל	wash, fuller	כבס
violence, injure	חמס	abundant	כבר
rise, ferment	חמר	lamb	כבש
five	חמש	trample	כבש
embalm	חנט	lie, decieve	כזב
dedicate	חנך	heep back, conceal	כחד
kindness	חסד	fail, false, lie	כחש
want, be without	חסר	dog, bark, basket	כלב
bend, incline	חפץ	shame	כלם
enclose, village	חצר	bow down, subdue	כנע
search	חקר	wind, corner	כנף
dry, wasted	חרב	harp, lyre	כנר
trembled, fear	חרד	fool, inward part	כסל
flat nose, devoted	חרם	desire, silver	כסף
autumn, scorn	חרף	cover	כפר
sharp, wound	חרץ	vineyard	כרם
plow, engrave, silent	חרש	bow down	כרע
think	חשב	cut	כרת
restrain	חשך	totter, stumble	כשל
dark, obsure	חשך	write	כתב
ornament	חשן	shoulder	כתף
seal up, finish	חתם	crown, surround	כתר
marry	חתן	white	לבן
slaughter, kill	טבח	dress, garment	לבש
sink, eminence	טבע	eat, battle, bread	לחם
hide	טמן	press, squeeze	לחץ

Learn to Read Biblical Hebrew

English	Root	English	Root
take, catch	לכד	vow	נדר
learn, teach	למד	seperate, withdraw	נזר
mock, scorn	לעג	obtain, possess	נחל
take	לקח	sigh, comfort	נחם
collect, gather	לקט	serpent	נחש
join, attack	לשך	settle, establish	נטע
tongue, speech	לשן	watch, gaurd, retain	נטר
rain	מטר	leave, abandon	נטש
sell, deliver	מכר	opposite	נכח
salt	מלח	strange, alien	נכר
deliver, eggs	מלט	pour out	נסך
reign, king	מלך	cover	נסך
present, offering	מנח	pull, break up/out	נסע
restrain, withhold	מנע	tie, fasten	נעל
mix	מסך	pleasent, agreeable	נעם
perverse, treachery	מעל	shake	נער
rebel	מרד	fall	נפל
smear, anoint	משח	break into pieces	נפץ
draw out/away/in	משך	set, place, erect	נצב
rule	משל	innocent, faithful	נצח
look	נבט	strip, snatch, take	נצל
wither, fade, foolish	נבל	gaurd	נצר
dry, desert, south	נגב	branch	נצר
declare, tell, show	נגד	spot, speck	נקד
instrument, song	נגן	avenge, revenge	נקם
touch	נגע	go, come around	נקף
strike, smite	נגף	reach, overtake	נשג
approach, brought	נגש	bite, usury	נשך
willing, impell	נדב	arm, battle, arrange	נשק
impell, expell, thrust	נדח	saw	נשר

English	Root	English	Root
give	נתן	heel	עקב
break out	נתע	exchange	ערב
tear, break down	נתץ	evening, raven	ערב
pluck, draw away	נתק	order, prepare	ערך
fold together	סבך	uncircumsiced	ערל
carry, burden	סבל	cunning, subtle	ערם
shut	סגר	heap	ערם
travel, go about	סחר	drop, cloud	ערף
foolish	סכל	turn the neck	ערף
forgive	סלח	fear, tremble	ערץ
flour	סלת	green herb	עשב
lean, lay	סמך	smoke	עשן
mourn, lament	ספד	oppress, violence	עשק
write, scroll	ספר	ten	עשר
castrate	סרס	smooth, polish	עשת
hide, conceal	סתר	ready, prepare	עתד
work, serve	עבד	meet, occure, attack	פגע
twist, weave, round	עבת	weary, exhausted	פגר
roll, revolve	עגל	tremble, fear	פחד
order, arrange, flock	עדר	escape	פלט
help	עזר	leap, limp, hop	פסח
surround, crown	עטר	cut, hew, idol	פסל
hide, eternity	עלם	work, wages	פעל
stand	עמד	impel, urge, move	פעם
labor, toil, mischief	עמל	visit	פקד
deep, profound	עמק	seperate, divide	פרד
earth, dust	עקר	sprout, blossom	פרח
suffer, pain, grieve	עצב	oppress	פרך
close, strong, bone	עצם	break, divide	פרס
restrain, detain	עצר	break, scatter	פרץ

Learn to Read Biblical Hebrew

English	Root	English	Root
break, crush, tear	פרק	cut	קרש
scatter, decide	פרש	attend, listen	קשב
strip, pull off	פשט	bind, tie	קשר
rebel, sin	פשע	lie with, copulate	רבע
flax, wick, linen	פשת	four	רבע
open	פתח	lie down	רבץ
sudden	פתע	shake, tremble	רגז
righteous	צדק	foot, walk	רגל
pass over, prosper	צלח	tremble,sudden	רגע
side	צלע	follow after, chase	רדף
spring, grow up	צמח	wide, spacious	רחב
cry out, assemble	צעק	mercy, compassion	רחם
small, young	צער	wash, bathe	רחץ
turn, leap, goat, bird	צפר	distant	רצק
leprosy, wasp	צרע	ride, rider	רכב
refine	צרף	go about, trade	רכל
collect, company	קבץ	get, gain, acquire	רכש
bury, sepulcher	קבר	tread	רמס
precede, early, east	קדם	creep, reptile	רמש
seperated, devout	קדש	hungry	רעב
little, small	קטן	shake, tremble	רעש
burn	קטר	murder, slay	רצח
bind, join	קטר	stamp, spread out	רקע
sling, cut/cast out	קלע	wicked	רשע
divination	קסם	staff, tribe	שבט
anger	קצף	flow, hair, robe	שבל
draw or come near	קרב	satisfy, fill	שבע
bald	קרח	seven, swear	שבע
horn	קרן	break	שבר
tear, rend	קרע	cease, rest	שבת

English	Root	English	Root
raise, high	שׂגב	measure, horrible	שׁער
give presents, bribe	שׁחד	fear, storm, hair	שׂער
slaughter, kill	שׁחט	family	שׁפח
lion	שׁחל	judge, justice	שׁפט
laugh, scorn	שׁחק	pour out	שׁפך
bruise, pound	שׁחק	low	שׁפל
black, early, dusk	שׁחר	bright, pleasent	שׁפר
corrupt, destroy	שׁחת	rest, quiet	שׁקט
adversary, hostile	שׂטן	weigh, weight	שׁקל
wash, overflow	שׁטף	cover, covering	שׁקף
write	שׁטר	loath, pollute	שׁקץ
lay down, layer	שׁכב	lie, false	שׁקר
forget, neglect	שׁכח	remnant	שׂרד
childless	שׁכל	burn, consume	שׂרף
act wisely	שׂכל	swarm, abound	שׁרץ
shoulder, journey	שׁכם	hiss	שׁרק
rest, dwell	שׁכן	weave, comb	שׂרק
drink full, intoxicate	שׁכר	root,spring up,origin	שׁרשׁ
bribe, hire, wage	שׂכר	weigh, ponder	תכן
send	שׁלח	palm tree	תמד
throw	שׁלך	abhore, abomination	תעב
entire, complete	שׁלם	strike, nail, note	תקע
draw or pull out	שׁלף		
three	שׁלשׁ		
destroy	שׁמד		
fat	שׁמן		
hear, obey	שׁמע		
gaurd, protect	שׁמר		
sun, windows	שׁמשׁ		
lean, rest	שׁען		

CPSIA information can be obtained
at www.ICGtesting.com
Printed in the USA
BVHW092047270722
643120BV00001B/130